Set design by Bill Forrester   Costume design by David Kay Mickelsen   Photo by Tim Fuller

Victor Talmadge as Doctor Watson, Mark Capri as Sherlock Holmes and Preston Maybank as King of Bohemia in the Arizona Theatre Company production of *Sherlock Holmes: The Final Adventure*.

SHERLOCK HOLMES:
THE FINAL ADVENTURE

BY STEVEN DIETZ

BASED ON THE ORIGINAL 1899 PLAY BY
WILLIAM GILLETTE AND ARTHUR CONAN DOYLE

★

DRAMATISTS
PLAY SERVICE
INC.

SHERLOCK HOLMES: THE FINAL ADVENTURE
Copyright © 2007, Steven John Dietz

All Rights Reserved

CAUTION: Professionals and amateurs are hereby warned that performance of SHERLOCK HOLMES: THE FINAL ADVENTURE is subject to payment of a royalty. It is fully protected under the copyright laws of the United States of America, and of all countries covered by the International Copyright Union (including the Dominion of Canada and the rest of the British Commonwealth), and of all countries covered by the Pan-American Copyright Convention, the Universal Copyright Convention, the Berne Convention, and of all countries with which the United States has reciprocal copyright relations. All rights, including without limitation professional/amateur stage rights, motion picture, recitation, lecturing, public reading, radio broadcasting, television, video or sound recording, all other forms of mechanical, electronic and digital reproduction, transmission and distribution, such as CD, DVD, the Internet, private and file-sharing networks, information storage and retrieval systems, photocopying, and the rights of translation into foreign languages are strictly reserved. Particular emphasis is placed upon the matter of readings, permission for which must be secured from the Author's agent in writing.

The English language stock and amateur stage performance rights in the United States, its territories, possessions and Canada for SHERLOCK HOLMES: THE FINAL ADVENTURE are controlled exclusively by DRAMATISTS PLAY SERVICE, INC., 440 Park Avenue South, New York, NY 10016. No professional or nonprofessional performance of the Play may be given without obtaining in advance the written permission of DRAMATISTS PLAY SERVICE, INC., and paying the requisite fee.

Inquiries concerning all other rights should be addressed to Sterling Standard, L.L.C., 445 West 23rd Street, Suite 1E, New York, NY 10011. Attn: Sarah Jane Leigh.

SPECIAL NOTE
Anyone receiving permission to produce SHERLOCK HOLMES: THE FINAL ADVENTURE is required to give credit to the Author as sole and exclusive Author of the Play on the title page of all programs distributed in connection with performances of the Play and in all instances in which the title of the Play appears for purposes of advertising, publicizing or otherwise exploiting the Play and/or a production thereof. The name of the Author must appear on a separate line, in which no other name appears, immediately beneath the title and in size of type equal to 50% of the size of the largest, most prominent letter used for the title of the Play. No person, firm or entity may receive credit larger or more prominent than that accorded the Author. The billing must appear as follows:

SHERLOCK HOLMES: THE FINAL ADVENTURE
by
Steven Dietz

Based on the original 1899 play by William Gillette and Arthur Conan Doyle

The following acknowledgment must appear on the title page in all programs distributed in connection with performances of the Play:

The world premiere of SHERLOCK HOLMES: THE FINAL ADVENTURE
was commissioned and produced by Arizona Theatre Company,
David Ira Goldstein, Artistic Director; Jessica L. Andrews, Managing Director.

for Glenn Bruner

AUTHOR'S NOTE

To be clear: I am no expert on Sherlock Holmes. I'm a writer of plays. I take stories and try to provide a blueprint for how they might be spoken and enacted onstage. But, having been asked to write a few words about the remarkable world which Arthur Conan Doyle invented — a world that I have been traveling in, of late — I offer these thoughts with humility to the Holmes experts and neophytes alike.

Much of the popularity of Sherlock Holmes, in my opinion, seems to revolve around one simple and enduring fact: it's fun to see someone get *caught;* to see the truth be found out. And only in these Conan Doyle stories, it seems, is the truth so immutable, so resolute, so imminently findable. The truth in Holmes is elusive, but is never subject to debate. How refreshing this is in an age where "truth" is a word that comes in plural form; where, in any twenty-four-hour news cycle, many conflicting "truths" are presented about the exact same issue — leaving us hungry for one person to stand up and say: "Nonsense. All of it. Here's the nub of the matter." Enter Sherlock Holmes.

Though groundbreaking in their day, these are not what we would call "modern" stories — they do not celebrate ambiguity and the gray areas of the human heart. These are proudly and unapologetically archetypal stories — emerging from the formidable shadow of Dickens and Poe — stories in which bad people do bad things and good people suffer and a coolly rational detective, armed with little more than guile and wit, solves the crime.

Then why do they last? Perhaps because we remember the man first, then the stories. Holmes, the man, is as complex as his cases are simple. He is "modern" in the extreme. He craves adventure, solitude, escape and elation. He is anxious, moody, vain, opinionated, caustic and empirical. He could wipe the floor with Donald Trump.

What's more, in Conan Doyle's most ingenious device, these stories of detection are built not on the slippery slope of crime — but on the enduring bedrock of friendship. As a playwright whose fundamental task is to make one's characters necessary to each other, Sherlock Holmes and Doctor Watson are a dream come true.

Literature has few rivals for the heady, imperious Holmes and the great-hearted, long-suffering Watson. These men are necessary to each other in the extreme, and their friendship — in all its colors, contradictions and complexities — is, to my mind, Conan Doyle's singular and lasting achievement.

The stories, then, last the way a friendship lasts: because they are at once familiar and unforgettable. They stay with us through days both remarkable and mundane, adventures grand and forgotten; through love and loss and a thousand wonderful conversations about nothing at all. All that Conan Doyle requires of us is that we take that first step, turn that first page, and enter in.

The game is afoot. Enjoy.

Steven Dietz
February 2006
Tucson

SHERLOCK HOLMES: THE FINAL ADVENTURE received its world premiere by the Arizona Theatre Company (David Ira Goldstein, Artistic Director; Jessica L. Andrews, Managing Director) in Tucson, Arizona, on March 10, 2006. It was directed by David Ira Goldstein; the set design was by Bill Forrester; the costume design was by David Kay Mickelsen; the lighting design was by Dennis Parichy; the original music was by Roberta Carlson; the sound design was by Brian Jerome Peterson; and the stage manager was Glenn Bruner. The cast was as follows:

SHERLOCK HOLMES	Mark Capri
DOCTOR WATSON	Victor Talmadge
PROFESSOR MORIARTY	Laurence Ballard
THE KING OF BOHEMIA	Preston Maybank
IRENE ADLER	Libby West
JAMES LARRABEE	Kenneth Merckx, Jr.
MADGE LARRABEE	Erin Bennett
SID PRINCE	Roberto Guajardo
ENSEMBLE	H. Michael Croner, Jonathan Hicks

This production transferred to the Pasadena Playhouse (Sheldon Epps, Artistic Director) in Pasadena, California, where it opened on May 5, 2006.

CHARACTERS

SHERLOCK HOLMES

DOCTOR WATSON

PROFESSOR MORIARTY

THE KING OF BOHEMIA

IRENE ADLER

JAMES LARRABEE (a.k.a. GODFREY NORTON)

MADGE LARRABEE (a.k.a. MARIE)

SID PRINCE (this actor may also double as: POSTBOY, CLERGYMAN, POLICEMAN, YOUNG SWISS MAN)

PLACE

London. And the Continent.

TIME

1893.

PRIMARY SETTINGS

Sherlock Holmes' study on Baker Street. The sitting room of Briony Lodge. The gas chamber at Stepney.

Please Note: This play was devised with the notion that all settings be suggested, not fully depicted. There is no need, for example, to render Holmes' study in full. A few pieces of furniture should suffice for each locale, allowing nearly immediate movement from one scene to the next.

Education never ends, Watson.
It is a series of lessons with the greatest for the last.

—Sherlock Holmes

SHERLOCK HOLMES: THE FINAL ADVENTURE

ACT ONE

A London street. Before dawn. The lamps are still lit. Fog blankets the street. A policeman emerges from the fog, walking briskly, rubbing his hands together for warmth. Suddenly, he is startled by the voice of a man.

MAN WITH PAPER. *(Working-class accent.)* Did ya hear, then?
POLICEMAN. *(Stops.)* Who's there? *(The man with paper is now slightly more visible, standing beneath the eerie glow of a lamppost. The man wears a dark coat and cap — and he is reading a newspaper, which conceals his face.)*
MAN WITH PAPER. It's 'ere in the paper. Want to see?
POLICEMAN. See what?
MAN WITH PAPER. Had it coming, you ask me. Made a lot of enemies in his day.
POLICEMAN. Who are you talking about?
MAN WITH PAPER. The Great Detective. The Bloodhound of Baker Street.
POLICEMAN. You mean Holmes?
MAN WITH PAPER. 'Ere —
POLICEMAN. You mean Sherlock Holmes?
MAN WITH PAPER. — Take a look. *(The policeman looks at the newspaper, as — Watson appears, opposite.)*
POLICEMAN. I won't believe it!
MAN WITH PAPER. It's all there —
POLICEMAN. "Dead and vanished — his body never found."
MAN WITH PAPER. — Right there in black an' white. *(The policeman lifts his head from the paper — and sees Watson.)*

POLICEMAN. *(To Watson.)* It's in the papers! Sherlock Holmes — he's dead! *(The policeman rushes off, as lights now isolate — Watson, alone. He speaks to the audience.)*

WATSON. It is with a heavy heart that I take up my pen to write these last words about the best and wisest man I have ever known. My friend. Mr. Sherlock Holmes. It had been six months since last I'd seen Holmes. Word had it that he was living a solitary life — his days spent amid his books in the rooms on Baker Street. Soon, however, he would undertake the final case of his remarkable career. And I would be there, once again, at his side — to the very end. Events began with the arrival of a letter. *(A postboy enters, saying —)*

POSTBOY. Are you Doctor Watson?

WATSON. Yes. *(The postboy hands Watson a letter, as — music plays: A soprano voice, singing a heartbreaking aria, and — light discovers Holmes, standing immediately beside a phonograph.)*

HOLMES. My dear Watson, it has been far too long since I've had the pleasure of your company. Please join me here at Baker Street tonight. It is a matter of some urgency. I shall expect you just before midnight — and I trust it won't trouble you to scramble over the back garden wall and enter through the cellar. Till then, please greet Mrs. Watson for me, and know that I remain very truly yours ...

WATSON. *(Turning to Holmes.)* ... "Sherlock Holmes." *(Holmes' study. Baker Street.)*

HOLMES. My dear Watson, good evening.

WATSON. Good evening.

HOLMES. Your first question involves the late hour I've summoned you, the absence of any servants to see you in, and the need to scurry over my fence like a ferret.

WATSON. Something along those lines, yes.

HOLMES. All will be explained, dear friend. All in due time. *(Watson removes his cloak and hat.)* Wedlock suits you, Watson.

WATSON. It does, in fact.

HOLMES. I believe you've put on seven and a half pounds since last I saw you.

WATSON. Seven.

HOLMES. Indeed, I should think it's just a little more than that.

WATSON. No. Seven exactly.

HOLMES. What is there, in your pocket?

WATSON. *(Remembering it.)* What? — Oh, yes — *(Watson removes a small garden trowel from a pocket of his pants.)* — I grabbed this in the garden. The cellar door was quite stuck. *(Watson hands the trowel*

to Holmes.)
HOLMES. There we are. Seven exactly. *(The aria reaches a dramatic crescendo. Holmes closes his eyes.)* Ahhh ... do you hear it, Watson? Do you hear that voice?
WATSON. Glorious.
HOLMES. It speaks to me in a sound which is seemingly beyond reason. What I hear in that voice, Watson, is not the fierce precision of music — but the incomparable sound of ...
WATSON. Love. *(Holmes opens his eyes, looks at Watson —)*
HOLMES. Nonsense. *(— And then quickly turns the phonograph off. Holmes opens his silver cigarette case, offering it to Watson.)* Cigarette, Watson?
WATSON. No. Thank you.
HOLMES. And Mrs. Watson, how long will she be away?
WATSON. Only a fortnight. She's visiting her — *(Stops.)* Wait. How do you know she is gone?
HOLMES. How do I know anything? How do I know that you've recently resumed the practice of medicine, gone for a country walk in bad weather, hired a careless servant girl, and moved your dressing table to the other side of the room? *(Before Watson can speak.)* Oh, don't look so dumbfounded, Watson.
WATSON. But, how could you surmise all that?!
HOLMES. Too simple to talk about. There is a bulge on the side of your tophat where you clearly conceal your stethoscope — to say nothing of the faint smell of iodoform, a known antiseptic. Only a dullard would fail to mark you as an active medical man.
WATSON. Yes, but what of the —
HOLMES. What's more, I see six nearly parallel cuts on the inside of your left shoe — where a particularly malignant servant girl has clumsily scraped round the edges, in a vain attempt to remove encrusted mud —
WATSON. *(Catching on.)* — From my long country walk.
HOLMES. Exactly.
WATSON. And my dressing table?
HOLMES. Your face is badly shaved on the right side. As long as I've known you, Watson, it's been badly shaved on the left. The light must be better on one side than the other — and since you couldn't very well move your window, you've obviously moved your dressing table.
WATSON. Amazing.
HOLMES. Elementary, my dear fellow.

WATSON. If only I could see what you see.

HOLMES. Oh, you see, Watson — but you do not *observe*. The distinction is clear.

WATSON. To you, perhaps.

HOLMES. *(Re: Watson's clothing.)* As clear as a missing waistcoat button, and yesterday's boutonniere in today's lapel.

WATSON. My wife is away.

HOLMES. *(Smiles.)* Yes, I know. *(A siren is heard, outside. Nearby.)*

WATSON. Some trouble on the street, I warrant. *(Watson goes to a window and begins to open the curtains.)*

HOLMES. If you please, Watson — do not open the curtains.

WATSON. I simply wished to —

HOLMES. *(More sharply.)* I must insist. *(Watson backs away from the window.)* We are here in secret, you and I. I've sent Mrs. Hudson home —

WATSON. For the evening, certainly —

HOLMES. For the duration, Watson. Till the game is ended.

WATSON. What game are you speaking of?* *[(Holmes does not answer. Instead, he retrieves a red case of Moroccan leather and brings it to his chair. He opens it and removes drug paraphernalia: a vial, hypodermic syringe, etc. He begins to fill the syringe.)* Which is it tonight? Morphine?

HOLMES. I'm back to my old love, Doctor. Cocaine. A seven-percent solution. Care to join me?

WATSON. Certainly not. I had hoped, in our time apart, that you'd stopped using these deadly drugs, Holmes —

HOLMES. Yes, Watson, I know.

WATSON. — For once these demons take hold of you, there is no end! The terrible ritual must go on, and on, and on. *(Holmes rolls up his sleeve, readies his arm for the syringe.)*

HOLMES. Like your ritual of eating breakfast must go on, and on, and —

WATSON. *(Forcefully.)* That is food, Holmes! Sustenance! These drugs are poisons — they will destroy you before your time.

HOLMES. Too late, Watson — my time has come. *(And Holmes injects the syringe into his arm. Closes his eyes. Leans back in his chair ... luxuriating in the effects of the drug. Watson looks away, then after a moment he approaches Holmes — lifts his wrist, checks his pulse.)]* Your wife is away for a fortnight, you say?

---

* It is permissible in performance to eliminate Holmes' drug use by disregarding the text between opening and closing brackets on this page.

WATSON. What? — Oh, yes, just a —
HOLMES. And your practice, is it busy at present?
WATSON. Nothing out of the ordinary —
HOLMES. It would afford you time to get away?
WATSON. Well — yes — certainly, if need be —
HOLMES. Oh, there is a need, Watson. I must ask you to come away with me for a full week — to the Continent. Will you do that?
WATSON. Of course I will — but why? *(Behind and above them [perhaps] is now gradually seen: an image of Moriarty. In one hand he holds a long-stemmed red rose; in the other, a pair of gardening scissors.)*
HOLMES. There is a man in London. A great, brilliant, and terrible man. His name is Moriarty. Have you heard of him?
WATSON. Never. *(Moriarty snips a stem of foliage from the rose.)*
HOLMES. And there is the wonder of him! He is insidious, Watson. He virtually pervades London — all that is foul and wicked, from Hammersmith to Blackwall, all of it is the work of Moriarty! He is the Napoleon of crime. *(Again: snip.)* He sits like a spider in the center of his web. If there is a crime to be done, a house to be looted, a man to be removed — you can be certain that Moriarty has authorized it. *(Again: snip.)* And though the agent who carries out the plan may be captured, the master himself never, ever leaves a trace. *(A final snip — as the image of Moriarty vanishes.)*
WATSON. He sounds monstrous.
HOLMES. I quite admire him — he's a professor, author, and abstract thinker. I can highly recommend his treatise on the dynamics of an asteroid.
WATSON. Still and all —
HOLMES. Without Moriarty, London would be a singularly uninteresting place.
WATSON. How can you say that?!
HOLMES. My days are sterile, Watson; my nights vanish without note. Audacity and romance seem to have passed forever from the criminal world — save for the grand malevolence of this good professor.
WATSON. Well, I for one am glad that he's met his match.
HOLMES. No, friend — I have met mine. *(Off Watson's look.)* Try as I might for nearly six months, it proved impossible to gain the evidence that would convict him. *(Beat.)* But then he made a slip. Only a small one — but from this slip, I began to weave together the various strands of his enterprise — over forty unsolved crimes — and trace them back to the man himself.

WATSON. So, you've done it, Holmes —
HOLMES. Yes —
WATSON. — Captured the spider within his own web!
HOLMES. — That is precisely what I was thinking as I took my evening stroll, and a pile of bricks came down from a roof and shattered at my feet — *(Sudden sound of this crash.)* — missing my head by inches.
WATSON. Good heavens —
HOLMES. And attached to this explicit projectile, a note. *(A light on Moriarty. He holds the rose.)*
MORIARTY. I know you, Holmes. I know every move of your game. You wish to place me in the dock; but I shall never stand in the dock. You hope to defeat me; but you shall never defeat me. *(Moriarty now places the rose in his lapel —)* You plan night and day for my destruction; but rest assured I am planning night and day for the destruction of *you*. (— *As the light on him fades away.)*
HOLMES. We are two men who share a shadow; our every move betrays us — one to the other.
WATSON. So, he's not been apprehended?!
HOLMES. Not yet. To succeed, the arrests of Moriarty and his men must happen all at once — all on the same day —
WATSON. Yes, of course.
HOLMES. — And the police require one full week to organize the plan. You and I must leave London at once, and not return until the arrests are complete — whereupon will follow the greatest criminal trial of the century. The game is afoot, Watson! — And it is a dangerous one. *(Handing Watson a note.)* For your own safety, you must follow my instructions to the letter. Now, make your way out through the pantry and exit by way of the coal chute.
WATSON. Yes, of course.
HOLMES. And should you change your mind — given your marriage and current happiness —
WATSON. I assure you —
HOLMES. — I shall not hesitate to travel alone.
WATSON. — My mind is made. *(Pause.)*
HOLMES. Very well. I should be lost without my Boswell. This may, in fact, prove to be a worthy case to document. For if I could rid this world of Moriarty — *(A loud crash is heard from somewhere in the building.)*
WATSON. What is that?
HOLMES. Go, Watson — do as I told you — *(And now: a series*

of loud sounds — pounding, things being upended —)
WATSON. What is the meaning of —
HOLMES. Now — for your own safety, make your escape — *(And now: footsteps coming down the hallway.)*
WATSON. *(Opening the door.)* They're coming this way — *(Holmes begins to casually load bullets into the chamber of a revolver.)* But they'll know we are —
HOLMES. The lamps, Watson.
WATSON. Right. *(Watson extinguishes most of the light in the room.)* But they've heard our voices —
HOLMES. The music.
WATSON. Right. *(Watson turns the phonograph on — turning the music up, loud.)* But where will we —
HOLMES. The desk. *[or: "Here."]*
WATSON. Right. *(Watson hides behind the desk [or elsewhere]. Holmes joins him, as — the door bursts open with a crash! A masked man stands there in the darkness — his presence is enormous, powerful, intense. He wears a brilliant cloak, fastened at the neck with an emerald brooch. Tall leather boots. The impression is that of "barbaric opulence.")*
MASKED MAN. HOLMES?! SHERLOCK HOLMES?! *(And now the masked man grows aware of the music. He moves inexorably toward the phonograph — and now his countenance undergoes a complete change ... he seems to weaken and grow smaller, and soon he falls to his knees and calls out [pronounced "Ireen-ee":])* IIIIIIIIIIII-REEEENNNEEEEEEEEEE! *(Another huge breath.)* IIIIIIIIIIIIII-IIIII ... *(Descends into sobs. Holmes and Watson peek out from their hiding places and watch, as — the masked man weeps, and slowly silences the music. The man lifts the cylinder from the phonograph and holds it lovingly. He closes his eyes and gently kisses the cylinder. But even as he is kissing it — his countenance is changing once again ... his body growing tense — his eyes filling with fire — and now he pulls the cylinder away from his lips — stares at it like a sworn enemy —)* Aaaaaaaauuuughghghgh! *(— And he hurls the cylinder to the ground and begins stomping it with his boots. Next, he makes for the fireplace poker [or lifts his sword, if wearing one], and — he proceeds to bash the cylinder into a hundred pieces as — Holmes addresses him.)*
HOLMES. I shall need that replaced. *(The masked man turns with a start.)*
MASKED MAN. Who's there?! *(Watson relights the lamps.)*
HOLMES. I might ask the same of you.

MASKED MAN. I am looking for the great detective, Sherlock Holmes.
HOLMES. Has he been invited to a *masquerade?*
MASKED MAN. *(Angered, confused.)* I sent a note to this address, informing Mr. Holmes that I would call!
HOLMES. My landlady is away — the mail has not been retrieved.
MASKED MAN. Yes, I know — I found my note on the doorstep! *(The masked man hands the note to Holmes — who reads it.)*
HOLMES. Since it is unsigned, whom might I say came to call?
MASKED MAN. I'm not at liberty to say. But you may tell Mr. Holmes this: My visit concerns a matter that may influence the whole of European history.
HOLMES. By which you mean the House of Ormstein, hereditary kings of Bohemia.
MASKED MAN. I've said no such thing!
HOLMES. It's all here in your note. *(Holmes hands the note to Watson — then settles into a chair and readies his pipe.)* Observe, Watson: the paper.
WATSON. Quite expensive, I should think.
HOLMES. The stationery of someone extremely well-to-do. And if one holds it up to the light — *(Watson does so.)* — one can see several letters woven into the paper.
WATSON. The monogram of its author?
HOLMES. Not at all. The "G" and small "t" are likely an abbreviation for *Gesellschaft* — which is German for "company." The "P," of course, stands for *Papier*. And now for the "Eg": I deduce it must stand for Egria — a small, German-speaking country in Bohemia, known for its glass factories and paper mills.
MASKED MAN. Astonishing.
WATSON. So, the paper was made in Bohemia.
HOLMES. And the man who wrote the note is German.
WATSON. How can you tell?
HOLMES. Note the peculiar construction of the third sentence: "This account of your skills we have from all quarters received." It lands on the ear like a boulder. That sentence could never be written by a Frenchman or an Italian.
MASKED MAN. *(It dawns on him.)* You are the man himself —
HOLMES. Only a German could be so uncourteous to his verbs.
MASKED MAN. — You are the great Sherlock Holmes!
HOLMES. And you are Wilhelm Gottsreich Sigismond von Ormstein, Grand Duke of Cassel-Felstein, hereditary King of

Bohemia. *(The masked man removes his mask.)*
KING OF BOHEMIA. At your service. Oh, what an honor this is! Your reputation, sir, precedes you.
HOLMES. As does, sir, your Bavarian cologne. This is my colleague, Doctor Watson.
WATSON. A pleasure.
KING OF BOHEMIA. *(To Holmes.)* I should prefer, Mr. Holmes, to speak to you alone.
HOLMES. *(Re: Watson.)* You may say before this gentleman anything you would say to me.
KING OF BOHEMIA. Yes, but were it not for —
HOLMES. *(More sharply.)* It is both, or none. *(Pause. Holmes moves away.)*
KING OF BOHEMIA. Very well. My case is of the utmost urgency.
HOLMES. *(Blithely.)* They always are.
KING OF BOHEMIA. In two weeks' time, I shall wed Clotilde Lothman von Saxe-Meiningen, second daughter of His Royal Highness, the King of Scandinavia —
HOLMES. You have my condolences.
KING OF BOHEMIA. — But, before I marry, I must put to rest a terrible scandal — a tawdry episode from my past which threatens to affect this union, and thus, the course of nations. You, Mr. Holmes, are my only hope.
HOLMES. That's very kind of you — and I'll have you know I'm a great admirer of the entire Carpathian region —
KING OF BOHEMIA. Thank you, sir.
HOLMES. — But owing to a matter of comparable urgency in my own life, I am taking no more cases at present. Now, if you don't mind —
KING OF BOHEMIA. *(Suddenly, with force.)* So it is true what they say? You are a thinking machine and nothing more?
HOLMES. I beg your —
KING OF BOHEMIA. Is it possible that your heart is so cold — so poisoned by reason — that you cannot hear that voice?!
HOLMES. What on earth does that —
KING OF BOHEMIA. *(Pointing to the phonograph.)* The scandal of my life involves that voice — that woman — that opera diva par excellence! *(Holmes stops, stares at the King.)* Her face, beautiful as nature's finest flower.
HOLMES. Do you mean to say —
KING OF BOHEMIA. Her mind, sharp as a knife.

HOLMES. —That the woman you speak of … is Miss Irene Adler?
KING OF BOHEMIA. Indeed she is. *(Beat.)*
WATSON. I shall check the index. *(Watson pulls out a long drawer filled with small index cards. He begins rifling through them.)*
KING OF BOHEMIA. Do you know her, Mr. Holmes?
HOLMES. Only from afar. I have long admired her performances.
KING OF BOHEMIA. Well, perhaps it's time you met. *(Holmes says nothing.)* The facts are these: Some five years ago, Miss Adler and I became romantically entangled. During the period of our affair, I wrote her some very compromising letters, as well as giving her a photograph. And now, as it happens —
HOLMES. As it happens, your royal wedding is pending and you are desirous of getting these items back.
KING OF BOHEMIA. Precisely. *(Holmes settles into a chair with his violin — sans bow. He begins to silently practice his fingering.)*
WATSON. *(Rifling through cards.)* "Abdication" — "Abyssinian cats" — "Accordions" — "Acrobatics" —
HOLMES. Tell me: Was there a secret pact between you and Miss Adler?
KING OF BOHEMIA. No.
HOLMES. Nothing signed by both parties?
KING OF BOHEMIA. No.
HOLMES. Then there is nothing to fear.
KING OF BOHEMIA. But what of the letters I wrote to her?
HOLMES. You simply claim they are inauthentic.
KING OF BOHEMIA. But what of my handwriting —
HOLMES. Forged.
KING OF BOHEMIA. My personal stationery —
HOLMES. Stolen.
KING OF BOHEMIA. My private seal —
HOLMES. Imitated.
KING OF BOHEMIA. And the photograph?
HOLMES. Purchased.
KING OF BOHEMIA. But, you see —
HOLMES. What I see, Your Majesty, is that there is no case here. Marry your Scandinavian nymph and think no more of it.
KING OF BOHEMIA. But the photograph is of both of us. *(Pause. Holmes lowers the violin.)*
HOLMES. Is it, by any chance, blurry?
KING OF BOHEMIA. Perfectly clear.
HOLMES. Are you standing apart from one another?

KING OF BOHEMIA. Arm in arm.

HOLMES. Amidst a crowd, perhaps? Thrown together on the street?

KING OF BOHEMIA. On the terrace of a remote villa, overlooking the sea.

HOLMES. Do you or she, at the very least, look ... somewhat ... *glum?*

KING OF BOHEMIA. We are the very picture of love. *(Holmes sets the violin aside.)*

HOLMES. Well, now we have something.

WATSON. *(Re: the index.)* There is nothing filed under "Adler." Nothing whatsoever between: "Actinium" and "Aerodynamics."

HOLMES. The photograph must be recovered.

KING OF BOHEMIA. We have tried and failed.

HOLMES. Then it must be purchased.

KING OF BOHEMIA. She won't sell it.

HOLMES. Stolen, then.

KING OF BOHEMIA. Five attempts have been made, without success.

HOLMES. And Miss Adler — she is aware of your impending marriage?

KING OF BOHEMIA. She has threatened to send the photograph to my bride's father on the day of the wedding. *(Pause. Then ... Holmes laughs.)*

HOLMES. Well, this is quite the three-pipe problem!

WATSON. *(Re: the index.)* You won't believe this: She was filed under "I" — for "Irene." Right between "Incandescence" and "Irritability."

KING OF BOHEMIA. How very fitting.

WATSON. *(Perplexed.)* Holmes, I have never known you to index a person under their first name. What could possibly have been the reason?

HOLMES. Clerical error.

WATSON. But —

HOLMES. Read the card, Watson. *(As Watson reads — music plays, and lights reveal: an image of Irene Adler — her arms extended, taking her bows, accepting the cheers of an adoring crowd.)*

WATSON. *(Reads.)* Adler, Irene. Born 1865, Sussex, New Jersey. Educated abroad. Triumphant debut at La Scala in 1887 —

HOLMES. — Which began her reign as the foremost operatic soprano in Europe.

KING OF BOHEMIA. Legendary performances in Paris, Berlin, Warsaw and Milan.

HOLMES. Her unparalleled Contessa in *Figaro*.
KING OF BOHEMIA. Her unforgettable Marguerite in *Faust*.
HOLMES. Sudden retirement from the operatic stage in 1891.
WATSON. Current whereabouts unknown. *(The image of Irene Adler vanishes.)*
KING OF BOHEMIA. *(To Holmes.)* You've followed her every move, it seems.
HOLMES. I admire her voice. Nothing more. *(Holmes kneels and picks up the shattered pieces of the cylinder.)*
KING OF BOHEMIA. And her face?
HOLMES. What of it?
KING OF BOHEMIA. You've not seen it?
HOLMES. I have her recordings. That is sufficient.
KING OF BOHEMIA. Do you mean to say you would not recognize her if you passed her on the street?
HOLMES. Her whereabouts are a mystery. It's there on the card.
KING OF BOHEMIA. There is no mystery, Mr. Holmes. She is here.
HOLMES. In London?
KING OF BOHEMIA. Briony Lodge, Serpentine Avenue, St. John's Wood.
WATSON. *(Re: the card.)* I shall make the necessary correction. Now: as Mr. Holmes informed you, he is at present taking no more cases — *(Holmes is now, inexplicably, grabbing a coat and hat.)*
HOLMES. *(To the King.)* Your wedding is in two weeks' time, you say?

KING OF BOHEMIA.	WATSON.
That's right.	Holmes —

HOLMES. Where?
KING OF BOHEMIA. A castle in the Swiss Alps.
HOLMES. Very well. I shall require three hundred pounds in gold to cover my expenses —

KING OF BOHEMIA.	WATSON.
Money is no object.	You can't be serious!

HOLMES. You must make yourself *completely invisible* — staying here, in this room, out of sight —
KING OF BOHEMIA. But the preparations for my wedding?!
HOLMES. By all means: Leave that to your bride. Nothing but agony awaits the man who involves himself in his own wedding.
WATSON. *(Strong.)* Holmes, this matter does not require your attention — the King is in no real danger here —

HOLMES. Know this, Watson: One of the most dangerous classes on earth is the drifting and vengeful woman. She inevitably incites in others their own latent criminality.
WATSON. But, we must leave the city! — You've said so yourself —
HOLMES. Listen to me —
WATSON. Think of Moriarty! — The threats on your life!
HOLMES. — I am thinking of nothing else. Time is short, Watson. And one final adventure is at hand! *(Watson, alone.)*
WATSON. Morning arrived, and Holmes set off for Briony Lodge — with yours truly racing after him. Once there, we encountered a man and woman rushing out the door and into the street. The man was calling for a carriage, and, upon securing one, he shouted to the driver —
VOICE OF NORTON. THE CHURCH OF ST. MONICA — AND DRIVE LIKE THE DEVIL! *(In the light from a cathedral window. Standing there, side by side: Mr. Godfrey Norton. And a woman wearing a dark veil, carrying a simple bouquet of white flowers.)*
WATSON. — Upon which, Holmes hailed a cab and shouted the very same thing. We reached the church immediately behind them — and watched as the man and woman emerged from their cab, and ran inside — whereupon they fell into conversation with a hastily procured clergyman. *(A clergyman joins them, and — Holmes has added a quick disguise: hat, scarf, etc.)* As we observed these developments in secret from the rear of the church, suddenly a voice rang out:
NORTON. *(Urgent, agitated.)* You there! You'll do. Come up here this instant!
HOLMES. I beg your pardon.
NORTON. We must have a witness — or it won't be legal. *(Holmes steps toward the others — taking his place next to Norton.)*
WATSON. Holmes was half dragged to the altar — and in no more than three minutes' time had successfully fulfilled the role of witness at the wedding of —
CLERGYMAN. Mr. Godfrey Norton. *(Norton puts his hand on the Bible.)*
NORTON. I do.
WATSON. — And a woman whose face he saw for the first time when she lifted her veil — *(The woman is angled to face Holmes as her veil is lifted. She is, of course, Irene Adler.)*
CLERGYMAN. Miss Irene Adler. *(Irene Adler puts her hand on the Bible.)*
IRENE ADLER. I do.

WATSON. *(Enraptured.)* And that face ...
CLERGYMAN. I now pronounce you man and wife. *(Norton and Irene Adler kiss, as — Holmes looks on, frozen.)*
NORTON. *(To Irene, intimate.)* Tell me your wishes. Whatever they are, I will —
IRENE ADLER. Take me away.
NORTON. Of course I will —
IRENE ADLER. Don't waste a moment. Complete our business and go directly to my home. I'll be waiting for you. *(A finger to his lips, a seductive whisper.)* Go now. *(Norton leaves, as — Irene turns to Holmes.)* How fortunate. Wouldn't you agree?
HOLMES. *(Blankly.)* Hmm?
IRENE ADLER. How lucky that you were here.
WATSON. To which Holmes managed to say ... *(Holmes is staring into her eyes.)* ... absolutely nothing. *(Irene holds out a small flower from her bouquet.)*
IRENE ADLER. Please — keep this. In remembrance of this day. *(Holmes does not take it from her.)*
WATSON. It was a white rose.
HOLMES. *(To Irene.)* The genus *rosa*. From the prehistoric Germanic of the Latin root — which many scholars believe derives from the Greek *rhodon*, of, perhaps, Iranian, or, failing that, uncertain origin.
WATSON. To which, Miss Adler said ... *(Irene stares ... then puts the flower in Holmes' hand.)* ... absolutely nothing. *(Irene Adler exits, as — Holmes turns to Watson.)*
HOLMES. That face, Watson. It is a face a man might die for. *(Holmes' study.)*
KING OF BOHEMIA. SHE HAS MARRIED SOMEONE ELSE?!
HOLMES. Indeed, she has —
KING OF BOHEMIA. I can't bear it!
HOLMES. — And please refrain from smashing my things.
KING OF BOHEMIA. And this new husband, who is he?
HOLMES. That is the question I posed to Mr. Norton's livery man today, under the guise of conducting a survey of airborne manure particles in greater London. I learned that Godfrey Norton is an attorney who met and consoled Miss Adler following her romance with a certain roguish nobleman. There followed a rapid courtship — bested only by the speed of the nuptials themselves.
WATSON. And now that she's married, she has no need to black-

mail the King — and we can be on our way —
HOLMES. But what of her new husband? Should the photograph fall into his hands, he too could use it against the King!
KING OF BOHEMIA. Oh, that's true! Where could it be?! *(Holmes merely shrugs, and moves away — toward a bureau or closet in the room.)* Can't you hazard a guess?
HOLMES. I never guess. It is a capital mistake. Now: Is the photograph small enough to wear as a locket?
KING OF BOHEMIA. No, in fact it's —
HOLMES. Therefore: She can't conceal it on her person.
WATSON. Perhaps she has entrusted it to someone.
HOLMES. I think not. Women are naturally secretive. I believe she has hidden it somewhere. *(Holmes has procured the collar, cloak and broad black hat of an amiable "country priest.")*
KING OF BOHEMIA. Somewhere far away?
HOLMES. No — very nearby. She's told us as much.
KING OF BOHEMIA. How?
HOLMES. She's threatened to send it on the day of your marriage — meaning it must be close at hand.
KING OF BOHEMIA. But where?
HOLMES. In her own house, naturally.
KING OF BOHEMIA. But we've had her house burgled a number of times.
HOLMES. Your burglars did not know where to look.
KING OF BOHEMIA. And you do?
HOLMES. Her new husband will tell me.
KING OF BOHEMIA. You think he knows?
HOLMES. Certainly not.
KING OF BOHEMIA. But how will you even gain access to the house? Do you expect he'll just invite you in?!
HOLMES. I suspect he will carry me.
KING OF BOHEMIA. *Carry you?*
HOLMES. Yes.
KING OF BOHEMIA. He will carry you into his home and tell you the secret location of a photograph that he has no idea even exists?!
HOLMES. *(A wry smile.)* Now, you've got it. Excuse me — *(As Holmes — now fully disguised — is crossing the room, he stumbles and falls to the ground, landing hard on his face — a pained cry:)* Aauuggghhh. *(— As lights instantly shift to — a lone chair in the room. Norton enters, hurriedly.)*
NORTON. *(Calls off.)* You hooligans! — STAY AWAY FROM

HERE! *(To Holmes.)* This way, Father! Let's get you inside! *(Norton lifts Holmes to his feet ... and carries him to the chair. Holmes' nose and face are covered with blood. He produces a white handkerchief and wipes the blood.)*
HOLMES. *(An Irish accent.)* I don't mean to trouble you ...
NORTON. Easy now — have a seat — I'll call for the maid —
HOLMES. Oh, you're too kind ...
NORTON. *(Calls off.)* Marie! The father needs a clean handkerchief!
HOLMES. Oh, it breaks a poor clergyman's heart —
NORTON. Pardon?
HOLMES. Those ruffians outside — grabbing for an old woman's purse —
NORTON. You should not have leapt into the fray, Father.
HOLMES. Have the police been called?
NORTON. There was no need — I dispersed them myself —
HOLMES. But, they may wish to —
NORTON. Please think no more of the police. *(Marie, wearing a maid's apron over her dress, enters. She hands Holmes a clean, white handkerchief.)*
MARIE. *(French accent.)* This is for you, Monsieur —
HOLMES. How awfully good of you.
MARIE. — And may I take your hat?
HOLMES. Oh, don't trouble yourself. *(Marie nods, steps away — but does not exit. She busies herself, nearby. Eyeing the room:)* Such a lovely home. Looks to have been in the family for years.
NORTON. Actually, it belongs to my wife.
HOLMES. Does it now?
NORTON. I've just moved in. We're newly married, Father.
HOLMES. Are you now? At St. Monica's, by chance?
NORTON. Yes, that's right.
HOLMES. With Father Murphy presiding?
NORTON. Yes, in fact —
HOLMES. Oh, God bless you, son — and I hope you won't mind a bit of fatherly counsel. In his home, a man needs a place of his own — a place to keep his *private things*. And his wife must know that, come what may, she is *never* to disturb this place.
NORTON. I take your point.
HOLMES. A man's secrets belong only to himself — and, of course, his God.
NORTON. Yes, of course.
HOLMES. Because no doubt your wife has a place like that —

women always do — and heaven help the man who chances upon her little pantry of discretion —
NORTON. In my wife's case, it is her music cabinet —
HOLMES. See there!
NORTON. — It holds her vocal scores and opera recordings — all locked away.
HOLMES. And all the better for you that they are. Now, tell me: How long has it been since your last confession? *(Irene Adler enters.)*
IRENE ADLER. How are you feeling, Father…?
HOLMES. … Hanson. Much better, thank you.
IRENE ADLER. *(Noticing the maid.)* Marie, that is all.
MARIE. Just finishing up, Madame —
IRENE ADLER. *(More sharply.)* I said: That is all.
MARIE. *Oui*, Madame. *(Marie turns and leaves.)*
NORTON. Father Hanson, are you familiar with my wife?
HOLMES. I regret to say I'm not.
IRENE ADLER. Godfrey, please —
NORTON. This remarkable woman was, at one time, the most celebrated singer in Europe —
HOLMES. I see.
NORTON. — Until a man she loved shattered her heart. She's never sung again.
HOLMES. What a great loss.
IRENE ADLER. Oh, the world is full of singers, Father. *(Irene is close to Holmes now. As Norton looks on, she takes the clean handkerchief from Holmes — and wipes a small bit of "blood" from his cheek.)* It is your work which truly interests me: to wrestle with the great questions — to confront the mysteries of each soul gone astray, and through cunning and diligence, to solve them. How I envy you that.
HOLMES. Yes, well —
IRENE ADLER. *(Brightly.)* Pray for me, won't you? *(And she is gone, as lights restore to Holmes' study. Later. Holmes is removing his disguise.)*
KING OF BOHEMIA. So the whole thing was an act?
WATSON. The London stage lost a great talent when Holmes devoted his life to the criminal mind.
KING OF BOHEMIA. But the blood?
WATSON. Just a bit of red paint —
HOLMES. Mixed to the proper consistency —
WATSON. And clapped to his face in the midst of the scrum!
KING OF BOHEMIA. But all the young hooligans?!
WATSON. The "Baker Street irregulars."

KING OF BOHEMIA. So, even the old lady with the purse — ?!
WATSON. *(A smile.)* One of ours.
HOLMES. It takes enormous planning to produce a random event. *(Watson, alone.)*
WATSON. Two nights later, under cloak of darkness, Holmes returned to Briony Lodge to retrieve the photograph. When next we saw him at Baker Street, he stood before us — his face ashen, his eyes fierce with wonder. *(Holmes' study. Night. Holmes addresses the men.)*
HOLMES. Upon reaching the sitting room, I went directly to the music cabinet. It was unlocked. And what's more: It was *empty*. No photograph to be found. I was about to slam it closed in disgust ... when I spied something. A small envelope, lying face down, at the bottom of the cabinet. *(Holmes produces the letter, as — a light reveals Irene Adler. Near her, a piece of luggage.)*
IRENE ADLER. Dear Mr. Holmes, you are as good as promised. Your disguise fooled my husband and the staff — but knowing the King would hire only the best, I suspected you from the start. One actor can never fool another. As I am not of noble birth, the King thought me unworthy to be his queen — and crushed me beneath his boot. Still: I regret nothing. I have no intention of blackmailing him — however, I shall keep the photograph as a safeguard; a weapon against future reprisals. *(During the following, Norton enters, lifts Irene's luggage, and waits nearby.)* For his part, Mr. Norton has married me for the woman I am, not the woman he wishes me to be. How rare to find that in a man. As you read this note, he and I shall be sailing to America, to begin our new life. Though you and I shall never meet again, Mr. Holmes, please know that I will forever remain, truly yours ... *(Holmes lowers the letter, saying —)*
HOLMES. ... Irene Adler Norton. *(Irene Adler and Norton leave, arm in arm, as lights restore to — Holmes' study. Quietly:)* I have, in my long career, been bested only four times. Three times by men. And now once — and only once — by a woman. *(Beat.)*
KING OF BOHEMIA. OH, WHAT A QUEEN SHE WOULD HAVE MADE!
WATSON. *(To the King.)* Still and all, it's done. You have the report you requested. *(Holmes moves away. He lifts the bow to his violin, and begins to soundlessly execute [sans violin] what must be a Paganini caprice.)*
KING OF BOHEMIA. So clever and resolute —
WATSON. Yes, indeed —
KING OF BOHEMIA. Such cunning — such bravery of spirit —

WATSON. Now, if you don't mind —
KING OF BOHEMIA. THE FINEST THING UNDER A BONNET ON THIS PLANET!
WATSON. — I shall see you on your way.
HOLMES. Do you presume, Watson, that Miss Adler knew I was aware of the photograph's location?
WATSON. *(Impatient.)* Of course — that's why she left her note for you in the cabinet.
HOLMES. Then why was the cabinet unlocked?
WATSON. She wanted to be certain you'd find it. Now —
HOLMES. But she would not want anyone *else* to find it — her husband, her maid —
WATSON. I take your point, but please let's —
HOLMES. — And what's more: If she wants me to find her note, why does she place it face down, at the bottom of the cabinet, where I may have missed it altogether?
KING OF BOHEMIA. Perhaps it fell.
HOLMES. Yes! Precisely!
WATSON. So it fell — that is incidental.
HOLMES. The incidental fact is often the most vital. I venture to say that Irene Adler, at the moment she had removed the photograph and was leaving the note to me in its place, at that moment she was surprised and accosted — the photograph taken from her — the note she'd written falling to the bottom of the cabinet — the door to which was hurriedly closed and thus left unlocked!
WATSON. But if that's true, why has she vanished to America with her husband?
HOLMES. *Has she?*
WATSON. It's all there in her note!
HOLMES. Written before she was apprehended. No, Watson — I deduce that she remains here in London under lock and key — a prisoner in her own home!
KING OF BOHEMIA. A prisoner of whom?
HOLMES. Of her marriage, of course! Of Mr. Godfrey Norton.
WATSON. You think he's not really a lawyer?
HOLMES. I fear he is that — *and more. (Holmes holds up the handkerchief.)* His true initials are here — given to me by a careless maid.
WATSON. *(From the handkerchief.)* "J. L."
KING OF BOHEMIA. He's not Godfrey Norton at all!
HOLMES. Open the index, Watson.
WATSON. Holmes, we haven't time to —

HOLMES. Now, Watson! Last name "L," first name "J." *(Watson searches through the index.)* It all fits, don't you see? The hurried wedding. The fear of the police.
WATSON. "Labyrinths," "Ladybugs," "Laplanders," "Larcenists" —
HOLMES. A name. We need a name.
WATSON. "Larkin," "Larouche," "Larrabee" —
HOLMES. Larrabee — that's it! First name?
WATSON. "James."
HOLMES. Read on.
WATSON. "Former legal counsel; swindler; rake; confidence man of dubious morals."
KING OF BOHEMIA. That's him!
HOLMES. Now, turn the card over and read the back.
WATSON. *(Reads.)* See also — *(Watson pauses. Looks up at Holmes.)*
HOLMES. Say it, Watson.
WATSON. "Moriarty."
KING OF BOHEMIA. So the marriage — the whole thing — is a sham?
HOLMES. An ingenious one at that. With your wedding only a week away — that photograph is about to fetch an enormous ransom.
KING OF BOHEMIA. And I'll pay it!
HOLMES. You'll do no such thing! We must use the power of that photograph to secure Miss Adler's freedom and capture her abductors.
KING OF BOHEMIA. You're speaking of using Miss Adler as bait?
HOLMES. I would never ask that of her.
KING OF BOHEMIA. Good.
HOLMES. *You, sir. You are the bait.* Listen now: You will take a room here in London under your own name. Make yourself *as visible as possible.*
KING OF BOHEMIA. But my wedding —
HOLMES. This will only take a day or two — during which time we shall root out an offer from Larrabee — and trap Moriarty in the bargain.
WATSON. *(To Holmes, furious.)* Give the police the week they need and they will capture Moriarty for you!
HOLMES. I seek that pleasure for myself.
WATSON. Holmes, why must you do this?!
HOLMES. *(Fierce, buoyant.)* Because it's delightful! Don't you see, Watson: My entire life has been a frantic attempt to escape from the dreary commonplace of existence —

WATSON. *(Sharp.)* That is not the reason and you know it! *(Off Holmes' look.)* It is her. The woman. She has done this. The thick armor of your emotional defenses has finally been cracked.
HOLMES. Nonsense.
WATSON. Your heart, at last, has overthrown your head.
HOLMES. WATSON, I SHALL SEE YOU IN THE MORNING. *(And Holmes storms out, as — lights isolate Watson.)*
WATSON. I met Holmes in the alley behind Briony Lodge. For his own safety, he moved through London on this day disguised as a horse groom. *(Holmes approaches Watson. He holds the clothing or cap from his disguise.)*
HOLMES. Good morning, Watson. Sleep well?
WATSON. I did not, in fact.
HOLMES. I slept like a child. Some cold beef, a glass of beer, and off I went.
WATSON. Once we are out of London and onto the Continent — then I shall rest easier.
HOLMES. Now, Doctor: I shall want your cooperation. I hope you don't mind breaking the law.
WATSON. Not in the least.
HOLMES. Excellent. There is only one point on which I must insist: No matter what transpires, you must not interfere. You must do nothing whatsoever to come to my aid.
WATSON. I am to remain neutral.
HOLMES. You shall wait outside the sitting room window, which I will open once I gain access to the house. When you see me raise my left hand — like so — you will throw this rocket into the room. *(Holmes produces a small smoke rocket from his pocket.)*
WATSON. A rocket?
HOLMES. A smoke rocket — nothing too formidable — fitted with a cap at each end to make it self-lighting.
WATSON. And I will throw this through the open window —
HOLMES. — While, at the same time, you shall raise the cry of "FIRE." Your cry will no doubt be taken up by many voices — but you must not leave your post at the window.
WATSON. Certainly not.
HOLMES. And when I raise my right hand — like so — you will blow this whistle. *(He hands Watson a small whistle.)*
WATSON. A police whistle, isn't it?
HOLMES. Exactly. After blowing it, you shall walk to the corner and wait for me. Is that clear?

WATSON. Remain neutral, stand by window, "left" for rocket, "right" for whistle, walk to corner, wait for you.
HOLMES. Precisely.
WATSON. I'm the man for the job.
HOLMES. Good old Watson — you are the one fixed point in a changing age.
WATSON. But, how will you know where to look for the photograph?
HOLMES. The woman will tell me.
WATSON. But if she is their captive, how will she speak?
HOLMES. She will tell me with her eyes. *(Holmes vanishes. Watson, alone.)*
WATSON. And he was gone. *(Beat.)* After making certain that the King was safely ensconced at the hotel, I did precisely what Holmes had asked — placing myself beneath the window at Briony Lodge, hidden from the street by a stand of bushes. *(Beat.)* It was only now, as I waited outside that dark, forbidding home, that I began to suspect the true danger of our situation. Suddenly — the window was thrown open, and this is what I saw: *(The sitting room at Briony Lodge. Morning. A once-elegant room, which now looks as though it has recently been torn apart by thieves. A huge safe is built into the wall or hidden by a rug on the floor. A staircase [perhaps] leads to an unseen second floor. Any visible windows have newly installed bars on them. Holmes — carrying a walking stick — speaks to "Marie, the maid" [aka Madge Larrabee, wearing a maid's apron and cap].)*
HOLMES. And this window, too, has bars on it. Recently installed.
MARIE. *(French accent, as before.)* Oui, Monsieur. It allows no one inside.
HOLMES. Nor out, I should think. *(Looking around.)* By the looks of it, the previous owners must have left in a rush.
MARIE. Oui, Monsieur.
HOLMES. Criminals, no doubt.
MARIE. Pardon?
HOLMES. The Nortons. They must have run afoul of the law.
MARIE. Oh, no, Monsieur. They were newlyweds. Left for the honeymoon in America and never came back.
HOLMES. And you, as their maid, were left to mop up after? *(Before Marie can answer.)* Speaking of which, you once lent me one of Mr. Norton's handkerchiefs — do you remember? —
MARIE. Impossible.
HOLMES. — But the handkerchief did not bear Mr. Norton's

monogram. Instead, it bore the initials: "J. L." Isn't that odd? *(Marie is frozen, staring at him. Brightly:)* Oh, well — mustn't blame the maid for the ills of the master. I'd like to see the kitchen and rear garden — *(And Holmes leaves, with Marie chasing after him, just as — Larrabee [aka Godfrey Norton] and Sid Prince barge through the front door, opposite. Sid Prince is dressed in a rough manner. He carries a leather bag filled with tools.)*

LARRABEE. Just get in here —
SID PRINCE. Like I said, I AIN'T NO SAFE-CRACKER — me dear pal, Colvin — God rest 'is soul — 'e was the safe-cracker.
LARRABEE. — Get in here and give it a try!
SID PRINCE. These were his tools, ya know — this was his bag — his widow give 'em to me at the wake —
LARRABEE. Yes, fine, whatever —
SID PRINCE. — An' she said the spirit of ol' Colvin is still right 'ere in this bag —
LARRABEE. The safe is over here —
SID PRINCE. — BUT SID PRINCE IS NO SAFE-CRACKER! *(Proudly.)* I'm a gun 'n cudgels man. An' I do a bit o' gassin' from time to time for the Professor — 'cause I'm his right-hand man.
LARRABEE. *(Livid.)* Get your right hand workin' that safe before my left hand's workin' your throat! *(They are now in front of the safe.)*
SID PRINCE. Look at the size o' tha' monster — how 'bout I jus' set some charges and blow 'er open!
LARRABEE. You can't blow up the safe! *(Sid Prince lifts his bag of tools and talks to it.)*
SID PRINCE. 'Ear that, Colvin? He won' let me do what I does best, which is scatter dead things about. *(Prince's bag seems to suddenly leap from his arms and fall to the floor. He stares at this event — both shocked and delighted.)* Why, HI-DEE-HO — HE'S HERE! *(To Larrabee.)* Ol' Colvin's gonna 'elp me crack it!
LARRABEE. Oh for God's sake —
SID PRINCE. *(With conviction.)* 'E'S HERE, I tell you! *(Prince immediately kneels before the safe, and gets to work, as — Madge rushes on, alone — dropping her accent and ripping off her maid's attire. She goes directly to Larrabee.)*
MADGE. He's here! Sherlock Holmes.
LARRABEE. What?!
MADGE. He's in the kitchen! Claims to be "viewing the property."
SID PRINCE. *(Calls to them.)* Are ya sure no one's got the combination to this monster?

LARRABEE. Only my wife knows it —
SID PRINCE. And you can't get it out of her?!
MADGE. Take me to her room: *I'll get it out of her.*
LARRABEE. No, Madge — none of that this time!
MADGE. It's all I ever do, James, is clean up your messes — *(Larrabee moves away.)* — all you had to do was swindle a singer, but instead you FALL IN LOVE WITH HER. *(Prince now wears a doctor's stethoscope around his neck, which he uses to listen to the lock.)*
SID PRINCE. Pipe down, wouldja?! —
MADGE. *(Furious.)* You had it in your hands! Right there at the music cabinet — but she bats her operatic eyes and YOU GIVE IT BACK TO HER!
LARRABEE. She wanted a final look at it!
MADGE. Mother was right: You're not worth a bucket of spit.
LARRABEE. Once we get the safe open, we'll have the —
MADGE. We don't even know it's in there!
LARRABEE. That must be where she put it! — We've searched everywhere — torn the house apart —
MADGE. *(Darkly.)* Moriarty will have your head for this, James.
LARRABEE. *(In a harsh whisper.)* This is not MORIARTY'S plan — it's MY plan.
MADGE. But I suppose the money's subject to the "usual division."
LARRABEE. He won't get a shilling out of me!
SID PRINCE. *(Working the safe.)* C'mon — 'at's a girl — here … we … GO. *(The safe opens. They all peer inside.)*
MADGE. EMPTY.

LARRABEE.	MADGE.
Impossible!	I knew it!

LARRABEE. That can't be — it's GOT TO BE IN HERE!
SID PRINCE. *(Calls into safe, makes an "echo.")* But it's NOT — NOT — NOT — NOT — NOT …
LARRABEE. SHUT UP, PRINCE. *(Prince laughs, packs up his tools, as — Madge starts off, fierce.)*
MADGE. I'll deal with your bride — YOU deal with HOLMES! *(Sid Prince instantly drops his bag of tools, as before.)*
SID PRINCE. *(Panicked.)* Wha's that you say?!
LARRABEE. Madge, no —
SID PRINCE. Oh, crap me out an oxbow! —
LARRABEE. — You must intercept him!
SID PRINCE. *(To Madge.)* — I HOPE TO GOD YOU DIN'T SAY —

MADGE. *(Wheels on Prince, livid.)* HOLMES. SHERLOCK HOLMES. HE'S IN THE BLOODY GARDEN. *(Sid Prince tries to rush out, just as — Holmes enters.)*
HOLMES. *(Brightly.)* Yes, the garden requires a bit of attention — but everything else seems to be in order.
LARRABEE. The house, Mr. Holmes, is not for sale.
HOLMES. You seem to know my name —
LARRABEE. *(Flattering him.)* Well, of course. Who doesn't?
HOLMES. — But I don't know yours.
LARRABEE. Norton. Godfrey Norton. *(Re: Madge.)* My sister, Margaret. *(Re: Sid Prince.)* My associate, Mr. P —
SID PRINCE. *(Quickly.)* Abernathy. *(Beat, re: the stethoscope.)* Doctor Abernathy.
HOLMES. A pleasure.
LARRABEE. Now, if I might —
HOLMES. You have my congratulations, Mr. Norton.
LARRABEE. Pardon me?
HOLMES. You're a newlywed, aren't you? Your sister told me that.
LARRABEE. *(Looking at Madge.)* Did she?
HOLMES. Of course, she failed to mention that she was your sister. In fact, she claimed to be your maid.

LARRABEE.	MADGE.
Yes, well —	I simply —

HOLMES. She also told me you were away to America.
LARRABEE. Just back this morning.
HOLMES. And your wife?
LARRABEE. Still there. I shall rejoin her in a fortnight.
HOLMES. I'm told she's quite the diva.
LARRABEE. And where did you hear that?
HOLMES. From your neighbors. Last night, in fact, they heard her singing — her voice ringing true and clear from an upper window. *(Pause.)*
LARRABEE. *(Sarcastically.)* You don't miss a thing, do you?
HOLMES. Occupational hazard.
LARRABEE. Think of it: the great Sherlock Holmes — here in our house — poking about for clues.
HOLMES. On the contrary, the truth is always out in the open.
LARRABEE. I expected more, frankly — from a legend such as yourself.
MADGE. *(Under her breath.)* That's enough now —
LARRABEE. I thought a master detective would have a few more

parlor games up his sleeve, Mr. Holmes.
HOLMES. Well, I'm sorry to disappoint you ... *Mr. Larrabee*. *(Beat, to Madge.)* And this must be Madge. It was Antwerp, I believe — where last I saw you. I remember your fondness for Belgian chocolates and German soldiers. *(To Sid Prince.)* And as for Mr. Sydney Reginald Prince — it will be my pleasure to reunite you with your colleague, Mr. Colvin.
SID PRINCE. Now, look 'ere, Mr. Holmes — *(With his walking stick, Holmes takes command of the room —)*
HOLMES. I have, in fact, looked here. *(He rattles the stick inside the empty safe —)* And here. *(He rattles the stick on the bars of the window —)* And here. And my inescapable conclusion is that there has been, in this house, an event of malevolent intent.
MADGE. Nothing could be further from the truth.
HOLMES. I wish to see your wife, Mr. Larrabee.
LARRABEE. My wife is away. I told you that. *(Holmes pushes his walking stick under a piece of furniture — and out slides ... Irene's luggage.)*
HOLMES. Then why is her luggage here — empty and unpacked?

LARRABEE.	MADGE.
Well, the fact is —	That proves nothing.

HOLMES. I am not leaving until I see her. *(Tense beat. Larrabee, Madge and Sid Prince all look to each other.)*
MADGE. *(To Holmes, flat.)* I'll tell my dear sister-in-law that you're here. *(Madge goes up the steps, as — Holmes settles into a chair.)*
HOLMES. Have you been to Bohemia, Mr. Larrabee? Wonderful country. I think you'd enjoy their King. Your wife certainly did. The two of them were the very picture of love. The King's to be married, you know. At a castle in Switzerland. I'm sure it will be a lovely wedding — and not nearly so rushed as your own.
LARRABEE. What does that mean?
HOLMES. "The Church of St. Monica — and drive like the devil!"
LARRABEE. You were there! *(Irene Adler appears. She looks weary and tense — but still luminous. Ever the actress, she does not reveal the terror of her situation. Madge is behind her.)*
MADGE. Here we are.
IRENE ADLER. My dear sister-in-law tells me you wish to speak to me.
HOLMES. For a moment, Miss Adler, if I may.
IRENE ADLER. *(After a look at Larrabee.)* My name is Mrs. Norton.
HOLMES. As you wish.

IRENE ADLER. You look tired, Mr. Holmes. You must take care not to end up an old man before your time —
HOLMES. Heaven forbid.
IRENE ADLER. — Some doddering old fellow like the good Father Hanson.
HOLMES. *(The accent from before.)* Kindly old Father Hanson. *(Larrabee and Madge realize ...)*

LARRABEE.	MADGE.
It was him ...	Wait ...

IRENE ADLER. And what of me, Mr. Holmes? Does marriage agree with me?
HOLMES. I should venture to say it does not. But, then again: You're no longer married.

MADGE.	LARRABEE.
How's that?	That's absurd!

HOLMES. I've been to the Hall of Records and renounced my signature. You therefore had no witness at your wedding. No witness: no marriage.

MADGE.	LARRABEE.
James — you idiot!	How dare you!

HOLMES. As to your health: You look pale. As though you haven't left this house in days.
IRENE ADLER. It's true. I have not.
HOLMES. And why is that? *(Irene looks at Larrabee and Madge.)*
IRENE ADLER. Because, Mr. Holmes, everything I shall ever need — is right here.
HOLMES. Of that, my dear woman, I have no doubt. *(Upon saying this, Holmes does the agreed-upon gesture with his left hand, and immediately — the smoke rocket flies into the room [unseen by the others], and — smoke begins to fill the room, followed immediately by —)*
VOICE OF WATSON. *(From off.)* FIRE! FIRE! *(There is a mad scramble — the smoke billows about — a fire bell begins to ring — and all is accompanied by repeated shouts of —)*

SID PRINCE.	MADGE.
FIRE! It's a FIRE!	The KITCHEN! Check the STOVE!

LARRABEE. GET WATER! GET A BLANKET!
ALL. *(Except Holmes and Irene.)* FIRE! *(Larrabee, Madge and Sid Prince all rush off, shouting, as — Holmes turns to Irene Adler just in time to see her staring with horror at one of the upholstered chairs in the room. She steps toward the chair and touches the back of it —)*
HOLMES. RUN FOR THE DOOR! SAVE YOURSELF! *(But

she does not run: She stops, staring at Holmes — caught. Slowly, she sits down in the chair, staring front, just as — Moriarty appears, his eyes on Holmes. He wears a rose in his lapel. One of his hands remains concealed behind his back, until noted. Similarly: One of Holmes' hands remains in the pocket of his coat.)

MORIARTY. "Save yourself" ... such good advice, Mr. Holmes. And, yet: how rare the man who is able to do so.

HOLMES. How rare, indeed. *(Now the fire bell stops ringing and the smoke begins to clear.)* A pleasure, Professor — though not a surprise — to find you here. I've been meaning to compliment you on "The Dynamics of an Asteroid." I found your conclusions astounding —

MORIARTY. Elementary, at best.

HOLMES. — And I was particularly struck by your theory of "change in the obliquity of the eliptic."

MORIARTY. It is, at present, an incomplete hypothesis.

HOLMES. Perhaps you'll have time to complete your work in prison.

MORIARTY. No, I think not. *(Beat, smiles.)* A dangerous habit, Mr. Holmes.

HOLMES. What's that?

MORIARTY. To finger loaded firearms in the pocket of one's coat.

HOLMES. Dangerous, as well, to hold a free hand behind one's back. *(Moriarty brings his hand out from behind him: It is empty.)*

MORIARTY. You think you can read me like a book.

HOLMES. No. Like a primer. *(Holmes sets his own gun on a table.)* There we are.

MORIARTY. To be clear, Mr. Holmes: I shall never be captured.

HOLMES. Not only will you be captured — but I shall testify against you.

MORIARTY. *(With a laugh.)* Impossible!

HOLMES. Though, I realize what an awkward position that shall put you in.

MORIARTY. And what position is that?

HOLMES. The one typically assumed by a criminal at the lower end of a rope. So tell me, what brings you to Briony Lodge?

MORIARTY. The lady of the house. As you know, our dear Irene once belonged to the King of Bohemia; then to Mr. Larrabee, or Mr. Norton, if you prefer —

HOLMES. This woman is an artist, Professor. And, being an artist, she belongs to no one person — she belongs to everyone, the whole of London —

MORIARTY. *(Nods in agreement.)* — Which means she now belongs to *me*. *(Moriarty reaches for an inside pocket of his coat, as — Holmes instantly lifts his revolver and points it at Moriarty.)*
HOLMES. I wouldn't do that, Professor.
MORIARTY. I was simply reaching for my notebook.
HOLMES. *(To Irene.)* My dear lady, if you don't mind: I wish to spare the Professor any unnecessary exertion. I wonder if you'd be so kind as to remove something from his left-hand coat pocket. *(As Holmes keeps the revolver trained on Moriarty — Irene Adler goes to Moriarty, reaches inside his pocket ... and removes a nasty-looking bull-dog revolver.)*
IRENE ADLER. Is this the item he's looking for?
HOLMES. Without a doubt. Put it there on the table, if you would. *(As Irene puts the revolver on the table — Moriarty makes an unsuccessful grab for it.)* Another inch, perhaps. Just another inch away. *(Irene moves the revolver, as directed.)* Very good. Shall we see if he has another?
IRENE ADLER. He's informed us that he does not.
HOLMES. Really, when?
IRENE ADLER. *(Re: Holmes' revolver.)* When he reached for that one.
HOLMES. *(Impressed.)* Precisely. Now, Professor: Is there anything more this good woman can do for you? *(Moriarty simply glares at Holmes. Holmes places his own revolver back inside his coat. Then — Moriarty once again reaches into his coat pocket, as before ... and produces a small notebook. During the following: Holmes lifts Moriarty's revolver from the table and casually inspects it.)*
MORIARTY. *(Consulting the notebook.)* You have a great deal to answer for, Mr. Holmes: You crossed my path on the fourth of January; on the twenty-third, you incommoded me; and now at the close of April you have tricked and betrayed and placed me in a position of continual persecution — the cumulative effect of which is the imminent loss of my personal liberty! *(Holmes restores Moriarty's revolver to the table.)*
HOLMES. Have you any suggestion to make?
MORIARTY. There can be but one outcome to this affair between us. *(Holmes now prepares his pipe.)*
HOLMES. And that would be?
MORIARTY. Inevitable destruction.
HOLMES. By which you mean: the destruction of you.
MORIARTY. You won't live to see that day!

HOLMES. Then may I live to see no other. For if I could be assured of your destruction, I should gladly welcome a similar fate. *(Holmes begins to light his pipe.)*
MORIARTY. Well, Mr. Holmes. That can be arranged — *(In an instant, Moriarty has grabbed his own revolver from the table — has aimed it at Holmes' head — and is "firing" it —)*
IRENE ADLER. MR. HOLMES! *(— But Holmes merely turns calmly, and continues to light his pipe, as — the last "clicks" of the revolver's hammer are heard, mere inches from Holmes' face.)*
HOLMES. Oh, look at that.
MORIARTY. *(In a rage.)* What the devil?!
HOLMES. I didn't suppose you wanted to use that thing again — *(Holmes reaches into a pocket and produces a handful of cartridges.)* — so I removed the cartridges. You're welcome to them. *(Holmes tosses the cartridges onto the table, casually, as — Larrabee, Madge and Sid Prince reappear, from various directions.)*

SID PRINCE.	LARRABEE.
There's nothing!	No fire to be found!

MADGE. It was likely Mr. Holmes. Some clever trick to drive us out of the house.
MORIARTY. Right you are, Madge. *(Moriarty turns to Irene Adler. He touches her face, tenderly —)* And it looks as though your new bride, Mr. Larrabee, will tell her secret to no one — not even Mr. Holmes. Therefore — *(Then suddenly produces a knife, which he holds to her throat.)* — we must provide some incentive.

MADGE.	LARRABEE.
Serves her right.	No, please —

HOLMES. There's no need. She's told me where it is.

MORIARTY. *(To others.)*	LARRABEE. *(To Irene.)*
Is that true?!	Impossible!

MADGE. She never said a word!
HOLMES. She didn't have to. *(Holmes sets his revolver down and goes to the upholstered chair. He pulls away a section of fabric, revealing ... the photograph.)*

IRENE ADLER.	LARRABEE.
Mr. Holmes —	That's it!

HOLMES. This photograph will now be returned to its rightful owner, and this terrible episode will be at an end.
MORIARTY. What shall be at an "end," Mr. Holmes — *(Suddenly: Sid Prince grabs Holmes' revolver and aims it at Holmes.)* — is you.
SID PRINCE. *(Giddy, to Moriarty.)* Wan' I should plug 'im one,

Cap'n?
MORIARTY. Not just yet.
SID PRINCE. *(To Holmes.)* Well — at least git yer 'ands in the air!
HOLMES. Very well. *(Holmes raises his left hand only.)*
SID PRINCE. And now the other one!
HOLMES. What's that?
SID PRINCE. YOU 'EARD ME. GIT YOUR RIGHT 'AND UP THERE TOO!
HOLMES. *(Beat.)* As you wish. *(Holmes raises his right hand, and — the police whistle is heard, loud.)*

SID PRINCE.	MADGE.
Oh, bugger me britches!	The police!

LARRABEE. They're right outside —
HOLMES. Indeed, they are. *(Police whistle sounds, again. Moriarty [who still holds the knife] gestures for Sid Prince to lower the revolver —)*
MORIARTY. You may leave, Mr. Holmes — but you will not be taking that photograph.
HOLMES. I had no intention of doing so. Its rightful owner ... is here. *(Holmes places the photograph in Irene Adler's hands.)*
MADGE. He's giving it back to her!
LARRABEE. You can't be serious! *(Irene Adler stares at Holmes — fearful, unsure what to do.)*
IRENE ADLER. Mr. Holmes ...
HOLMES. Go, now. You've nothing to fear. *(In silence, Irene Adler slowly walks past Moriarty and the others ... opens the door ... and is gone.)*
MORIARTY. You surprise me, Holmes. I was under the impression that you cared for that woman. Why, then, would you entreat her to leave the one place in London where she is safe? *(Fierce, to the others.)* OUT THE BACK! — FOLLOW HER! *(Larrabee, Madge and Prince all rush from the room. To Holmes:)* I sat with your dear Irene, earlier today — on her bed, our hands intertwined. And as I wiped a tear from her cheek, she spoke of you: "If only I had not deceived Mr. Holmes ... perhaps then he would come to my aid, and protect me."
HOLMES. That, Professor, is exactly what I've done.
MORIARTY. What you've done, Mr. Holmes, is sent the woman you love to her death. *(Upon this final word: Moriarty plunges the knife into the upholstered chair, as — lights rush to black.)*

End of Act One

ACT TWO

Holmes' study. Morning. Watson and Holmes are seated. The remains of breakfast are on the table. The King of Bohemia is standing: agitated, lost, confused. Holmes and Watson pay the King no mind, until noted.

HOLMES. The tea, Watson.
WATSON. Yes?
HOLMES. Weak.
WATSON. I'm sorry.
HOLMES. The eggs.
WATSON. Yes?
HOLMES. Hard as rocks. The sausages: improperly browned. And the toast, in seeming deference to the meat: burned beyond recognition. Oh, how I long for Mrs. Hudson — the comforting sound of her stately tread.
WATSON. I remind you that for her own safety you sent Mrs. Hudson home.
HOLMES. Yes — but do try harder this evening, Watson. I could not bear another meal like this.
WATSON. *(Happily.)* We shall dine this evening on the Continent. You've found the photograph; you've freed Miss Adler. Now we can get you safely out of London.
KING OF BOHEMIA. *(Trying to be calm.)* Pardon me, gentlemen. I wonder if I might be allowed to make ever-so-slight an interjection?

WATSON.	HOLMES.
Certainly.	By all means.

KING OF BOHEMIA. *(Beat, explodes.)* YOU GAVE IT BACK TO HER?
HOLMES. Exactly.
KING OF BOHEMIA. AAAUUUGGGHHH. *(The King collapses into a chair.)*
WATSON. So, that's an end to it. *(Watson stands, just as Holmes says:)*

HOLMES. I've had a call this morning, Watson — from Inspector Lestrade at Scotland Yard.
WATSON. Have they begun the arrests?
HOLMES. They will, presently —
WATSON. Just as you planned.
HOLMES. — With one exception: The authorities no longer have the evidence they need to convict Moriarty.
WATSON. Impossible! Only a day ago, they had all their witnesses lined up.
HOLMES. And they remain lined up. In a neat row. At the city morgue. A bullet here; a vial of poison there. The deep, unforgiving river.
WATSON. That's hideous.
HOLMES. And brilliant, as well. Each murder is untraceable — which means Moriarty must now be caught at a crime *in which he is personally involved.*
WATSON. But, the only reason he would involve himself in that way — *(Stops, beat.)* — would be to encounter you.
HOLMES. Precisely. I shall be the witness that convicts him.
WATSON. You can't do it, Holmes —
HOLMES. Listen to me —
WATSON. — You can't walk right into his trap!
HOLMES. — We are fortunate in this regard: Moriarty knows I'm involved in this matter with the King. *(Turns to the King.)* Therefore, Your Highness, we shall press on. *(The King suddenly looks up —)*

KING OF BOHEMIA.	WATSON.
What did you say?	Holmes, no!

HOLMES. Now: I took it upon myself to intercept your mail this morning.
KING OF BOHEMIA. You *what? (Holmes produces two letters.)*
HOLMES. This letter was sent to your hotel. The second was delivered here, by courier. A young man — slight build, fair of face, oversized cap. *(The King opens and reads the letters.)* The first letter, as you'll see, is from Miss Adler. She has — in the irrational manner of women in love — chosen to forgive you completely.
KING OF BOHEMIA. *(Looking at letter.)* I am to appoint Sherlock Holmes as my proxy. He is to fill a valise with five thousand pounds, cash — and then meet a carriage with wooden shutters, which shall take him, alone, directly to Miss Adler —
HOLMES. — Whereupon, in exchange for the money, she will give me the photograph — which I shall return to you.

KING OF BOHEMIA. That is best of all worlds!
HOLMES. Not so. The letter is a fake.
KING OF BOHEMIA.   WATSON.
What?!   But how do you know?
HOLMES. The reason for the shuttered carriage is clear: to make it impossible for me to know where the driver is headed. No — whomever sent this letter wants to put me fully at their mercy, and that can only mean —
WATSON. — Moriarty.
KING OF BOHEMIA. But, that's impossible!
WATSON. Why?
KING OF BOHEMIA. *(Holding it up.)* Because the second letter is from Moriarty! Why would he both *write* me a letter and *forge* me a letter?
HOLMES. The answer will soon be clear.
KING OF BOHEMIA. *(As he reads it.)* In this letter, he states ... *(Stops.)*
WATSON. What is it?
KING OF BOHEMIA. *(More quietly.)* ... He states that Irene Adler is dead. Murdered by one of his men.
WATSON. My God ...
KING OF BOHEMIA. *(Offering the letter to Watson.)* He claims he has the photograph, and will demand payment from me this evening ...
WATSON. *(Reading the letter.)* You're to wait for him. Here. Alone.
HOLMES. *(With admiration.)* He is truly a master of the game.
KING OF BOHEMIA. *(Distraught.)* Is that all you can say? My queen — my Venus — has been murdered and you feel nothing?!
HOLMES. Yes — the cruelty is complete! You abandoned her — Larrabee deceived her — and now Moriarty has destroyed her. Yes — these are the facts before us! These are the spoils of love!
KING OF BOHEMIA. But you must do something!
HOLMES. And you must do as the second letter demands: Wait here, in this room, for Moriarty.
KING OF BOHEMIA. And what of the first letter?! *(Holmes sets pen and paper in front of the King.)*
HOLMES. You shall write out a reply to Miss Adler —
KING OF BOHEMIA. Even though it's a fake? Even though she may be dead?
HOLMES. *(Dry.)* You really have no talent for this, do you? *(Before the King responds.)* You shall write out a reply as though unaware of

the other letter — telling Miss Adler that you accept her terms and shall send me with the money. *(Holmes produces a leather valise, as — the King begins writing.)* There's a bank round the corner. Have the full amount wired to you immediately — and place it in this valise.

KING OF BOHEMIA. But to where shall I post my reply?

HOLMES. Leave that to me. I will meet the carriage, as described — and before the night is out, I shall have your photograph.

KING OF BOHEMIA. And Moriarty will have my money.

HOLMES. No, I'll have that as well. *(Holmes grabs the reply which the King has written.)*

KING OF BOHEMIA. But if he doesn't get the money, he'll kill me! *(Holmes hands the King his cloak and the leather valise —)*

HOLMES. Yes — it may be quite unpleasant. Now: GET TO THE BANK THIS INSTANT. *(— And pushes him out the door.)*

WATSON. You never answered his question. Why the Professor would send two letters.

HOLMES. He wouldn't. And he didn't.

WATSON. Meaning?

HOLMES. They are *both* forged. The first letter, as I've theorized, was forged by Moriarty.

WATSON. And the second?

HOLMES. Forged by the woman. By Miss Adler herself.

WATSON. She's alive?

HOLMES. Oh, yes.

WATSON. But, for her own safety — why has she not left the city?

HOLMES. She is a woman, Watson. And therefore: She will never forget who has wronged her. What's more, she's a diva — and, as such, she lives for confrontation. Before she leaves London, she will set her sights on the two men who have broken her heart.

WATSON. And what of the third man? The man who saved her life? *(Holmes stares at Watson. Beat.)*

HOLMES. *(Handing it to Watson.)* Here is the King's note. Step outside and hold it in the air. I suspect a courier shall arrive within moments — slight build, fair of face, oversized cap.

WATSON. And where will he take it?

HOLMES. He shall keep it. For it is his. Or rather: *hers. (Off Watson's look.)* Yes — she's been following me — watching it all play out —

WATSON. While in disguise?

HOLMES. Yes —

WATSON. As a courier on the street?

HOLMES. — Awaiting the right moment to step forward.

WATSON. And you believe she still has the photograph?
HOLMES. Without a doubt.
WATSON. Then what will you be given in return for the King's money?
HOLMES. I won't be giving away the money.
WATSON. But —
HOLMES. I will be there to witness the crime first-hand; to hang this charge of extortion upon Moriarty — and the police shall do the rest. *(Holmes goes to a cabinet filled with chemical supplies.)*
WATSON. But there's something I still don't understand —
HOLMES. *(Re: chemicals.)* Here we are ...
WATSON. Why would you want Miss Adler to know our plan?
HOLMES. *(Ignoring Watson.)* ... These shall do nicely,
WATSON. Unless, knowing you're in danger, you believe she will come forward with the photograph! *(Holmes is mixing the chemicals in various beakers, etc.)*
HOLMES. *(As he works.)* Quiet, now — this is a delicate mixture —
WATSON. Or perhaps you simply wish to see her face.
HOLMES. *(With force.)* Do you really think, Watson, that I would put your life and mine needlessly at risk — all to secure the affections of a woman?
WATSON. That, Holmes, would be the greatest cause imaginable. *(Holmes stares at him — then returns to mixing the chemicals.)*
HOLMES. These chemicals are not to be disturbed for one hour — upon which time you will douse several large rags with the resulting liquid. When the King returns with the money, place these rags in the hidden compartment of the valise. Then close the valise — lock it — and bring it with you tonight, following my carriage in a carriage of your own. Is that clear?
WATSON. Yes, of course, but —
HOLMES. Now: I've learned through one of our lads on the street that Moriarty's driver will be taking me to the old Stepney Gas Works. You shall follow me there, Watson — wait exactly five minutes — and then enter the building.
WATSON. And if your carriage does not stop there?
HOLMES. Go straight to the police. Report my disappearance. Remember me fondly. And record my final adventure in your books.* *[(Holmes has retrieved the red case of Moroccan leather containing his drug paraphernalia. He holds it in his hands, staring at it.)*

---

* If the bracketed text on page 14 is disregarded in performance, it is also permissible to disregard the text between opening bracket on this page and closing bracket on page 47.

WATSON. And that — your seven percent solution — shall I bring that with me, as well?
HOLMES. Don't you see, Watson: *(Holmes tosses the case aside or to Watson, saying —)* I've no need for it now.] *(Watson stares at Holmes.)* By the way, do you still carry matches?
WATSON. *(Reaching for them.)* Yes. Of course.
HOLMES. Good. I shall see you tonight. *(Holmes leaves the room, briskly. Watson, alone.)*
WATSON. I stepped outside with the King's note, and no sooner had I lifted it into the air when — *(A courier in an oversized cap [presumably Irene Adler in disguise] steps forward. We do not clearly see his/her face.)*
COURIER IN CAP. *(Re: the note.)* To be posted, then?
WATSON. Yes … thank you. *(The courier takes the note and is gone.)* One hour later, the King returned — the valise now filled with money. "A royal ransom," as he called it, "fit for a queen." For my part, I doused the rags with the chemicals which Holmes had prepared — the smell of which nearly drove me from the room. I wrung them out, hid them inside the valise, as directed; then I posted a letter to my wife, Mary — telling her nothing of my exploits … only of my love. As darkness fell, a shuttered carriage pierced the fog. I watched as Holmes climbed inside — wondering all the while whether I'd seen the last of my dear friend. *(Beat.)* Then I hailed a cab of my own … and gave chase. *(The gas chamber at Stepney. A grim and brutal room — barren, except for a battered table and a single chair. An imposing door provides access. A smaller door leads to an unseen closet. On one wall, a large metal flywheel. Moriarty is walking about the room, inspecting it. He carries [and uses] a walking stick, very much in the manner of Holmes. Sid Prince follows Moriarty around the room, carrying an electric light of some kind. Larrabee sits in the lone chair at the table — nervous, tense.)*
MORIARTY. The last one, Mr. Prince — when did you do the last one?
SID PRINCE. 'Bout two days ago.
MORIARTY. That witness from the Underwood trial?
SID PRINCE. Ol' Bassick, you mean? — No, we gutted him.
MORIARTY. That swindler from the railyard job?
SID PRINCE. No — poor Craigen leapt to his death.
MORIARTY. *(Ice.)* Pity.
SID PRINCE. It was O'Hagan — the policeman who kept pokin' about — I gassed 'im real nice an' dumped 'im in the quarry.

MORIARTY. Hardly a trace of the smell left.
SID PRINCE. I aired it out real good. Don' want Mr. Holmes to know wha's comin', do we?
MORIARTY. And what of the lamp?
SID PRINCE. Electric. Completely safe. No flame at all.
MORIARTY. Very good. *(Larrabee puts a cigarette in his mouth, and reaches for his matches —)*
SID PRINCE. WHOA THERE! — D'ya want to blow us all into NEXT WEEK?!
LARRABEE. You said you aired out the room!
SID PRINCE. Yeah, but still —
LARRABEE. And you haven't turned the gas on!
SID PRINCE. Not yet, I 'aven't —
LARRABEE. So, I don't see what harm it would do —
SID PRINCE. It'll do NO 'ARM for sure if ya LIGHT NO MATCHES! *(Moriarty pulls the cigarette from Larrabee's mouth.)*
MORIARTY. *(Sharp.)* No mistakes tonight, Larrabee.
LARRABEE. Tell it to Prince — he's the one you should worry about.
SID PRINCE. Wha' the devil's that s'posed to mean?!
LARRABEE. It means what it means.
SID PRINCE. Well, aren't you jus' the poet.
MORIARTY. Enough —
SID PRINCE. Aren't you jus' the great silver-tongued romancer who could never manage to get a four-inch piece o' paper away from the li'l woman 'e married!
LARRABEE. *(Livid.)* How dare you say something like —
MORIARTY. He's right, Larrabee: That woman will prove your undoing. *(To Prince.)* You've got the rope to tie him with? *(Prince lifts a strong, coiled rope.)*
SID PRINCE. Done.
MORIARTY. And you're certain the room is airtight?
SID PRINCE. Tight as a drum, gov'nor. I caulked every crevice meself. *(Moriarty bangs his walking stick against the closet door.)*
MORIARTY. This door — any outlet here?
SID PRINCE. No, sir — jus' a closet. *(Proudly.)* I keeps me guns n' cudgels in there.
MORIARTY. No shooting. Do you understand? No matter what happens: No shot is to be fired tonight — it can be heard in the alley. And those high windows, what of them?
SID PRINCE. Spiked down, sir — not that any man could reach

'em, anyways.
MORIARTY. Mr. Holmes is not just *any man*. Underestimate him at your peril. He might break that glass —
SID PRINCE. — And smack right into the iron bars behin' it.
MORIARTY. Well, done. And the doorway?
SID PRINCE. Planked up solid. Double-thickness.
MORIARTY. And secured from the outside?
SID PRINCE. Two iron bolts and a 'uge metal bar. There ain't an army who could break it down. *(Moriarty approaches the large flywheel — attached to the wall.)*
MORIARTY. And this delivers the gas?
SID PRINCE. Tha's right, gov'nor. Three good turns and ya got all the gas ya could 'ope for. Gives out a sweet little hiss — like it's whisperin' "bye-bye" to the poor dyin' sod.
MORIARTY. But what keeps the victim from rushing over and turning it off?
SID PRINCE. I put a lockin' mechanism on it. Right 'ere. Three turns and it locks in place — an' the gas won't stop a-comin'.
MORIARTY. Excellent.
SID PRINCE. *(Grandly.)* I make it a point, gov'nor, to think o' everything.
LARRABEE. *(Can't stand it anymore.)* Oh, would you shut your measly trap!
SID PRINCE. Mighty tough words for a man who got outsmarted by a SONGBIRD. *(Larrabee stands — as Prince approaches him, ready to fight.)*

SID PRINCE.	MORIARTY.
(Rising to the bait.)	*(A reprimand.)*
There we are!	Larrabee!
	LARRABEE.
You wanta have a go?	I've had it with your "gov'nor
— okay, let's have a *go!*	this" and "gov'nor that" — you're nothing but a STUPID, PETTY THUG.

(At this: Prince wrestles Larrabee down onto the table, as —)
MORIARTY. DOGS! *(Moriarty, with seeming superhuman strength, throws Sid Prince off the table and across the room with one hand, and —)* IS THAT IT? *(— With the other hand, he uses his walking stick to pin Larrabee to the table by his neck.)* ARE WE NOTHING BUT DOGS?! *(Silence. Nothing is heard but the heavy, panicked breathing of Prince and Larrabee. Quiet, fierce:)* Here is

how it will go: Holmes believes he is coming to meet Miss Adler. You, Larrabee, shall have exactly two minutes alone with him, during which time you will explain that the photograph now belongs to us. You will make certain he has brought the money. And when Mr. Prince and I appear, you shall disarm him and tie him to this chair. I shall then give Mr. Holmes a proper send-off to the hereafter. *(Moriarty releases the walking stick, enabling Larrabee to sit up.)*
LARRABEE. And the money?
MORIARTY. I'll take that with me.
LARRABEE. That was not our arrangement!
MORIARTY. Our arrangement, Larrabee, was that all profits would be subject to the usual division.
LARRABEE. Yes, but I'm the one who —
MORIARTY. And in this case, the usual division means I take what I want and refrain from *killing you*. Is that clear? *(Larrabee stares at him.)* Two minutes. Not a whisker more. *(Moriarty and Sid Prince leave the room — closing, but not locking/bolting the door. The electric light is left on the table — casting an odd, lonely light upon — Larrabee, as he collapses into the chair — his head in his hands. Beat. Slowly, the closet door opens, and ... Irene Adler emerges. Walking quietly, purposefully — both hands behind her back — she approaches Larrabee, from behind ... until she is standing directly behind him. She brings her hands out from behind her back, and we see that she is carrying a revolver. She coolly lifts it and holds it to the back of Larrabee's head.)*
IRENE ADLER. For better ... *(Larrabee gasps; freezes.)* And for worse. *(Larrabee very slowly lifts his head from his hands.)* In sickness ...
LARRABEE. *(Weakly.)* Irene?
IRENE ADLER. And in health.
LARRABEE. How did you —
IRENE ADLER. Till death ... *(She cocks the trigger of the revolver —)*
LARRABEE. No! — Please!
IRENE ADLER. ... Do us part. *(Larrabee closes his eyes, tightly — expecting the gun to fire.)* Say: I do.
LARRABEE. *(A whisper.)* I do.
IRENE ADLER. I can't hear you.
LARRABEE. *(Louder.)* I do. *(After each question, Irene Adler nudges the gun a bit into Larrabee's skull, prompting him —)*
IRENE ADLER. Do you lie to me, darling?

LARRABEE. I do.
IRENE ADLER. Do you tell me your name is Godfrey Norton?
LARRABEE. I do.
IRENE ADLER. And even though your name is James Larrabee and you're a crook and a cad and a wanted man — do you capture and imprison me and sell me out without a second thought? *(Before he can respond.)* And do you know how that feels, James? How it feels to be heartbroken? And helpless? Completely and utterly helpless?
LARRABEE. *(Desperate.)* I love you, Irene! *(Irene says nothing. Instead, she slowly moves the gun around his head — then lifts his chin with the barrel, causing him to look her in the eye.)*
IRENE ADLER. And do you think that will save you? Because it won't, darling. *(A whisper.)* Do you know I'm going to kill you now and never think of you again?
LARRABEE. *(A whisper.)* I do.
IRENE ADLER. Good. *(Larrabee closes his eyes, as — Irene takes one step back, and tightens her grip on the gun, as though about to fire —)* I now pronounce us: man ... *(And now ... she lowers the gun and speaks with an odd, lucid calm.)* ... and woman. *(Larrabee slowly opens his eyes, turns to her — confused, scared. Looking around:)* Charming place, James.
LARRABEE. Irene, what on earth —
IRENE ADLER. It's simple, really: I followed you here. Snuck inside while you were chatting with your driver. And from that closet — I heard everything.
LARRABEE. Are you mad?
IRENE ADLER. I am the woman you've made of me.
LARRABEE. Do you have any idea what he'll do to you? — If Moriarty were to find you here —
IRENE ADLER. He won't enter before Mr. Holmes, remember?
LARRABEE. *(A threat.)* He will if I call for him.
IRENE ADLER. *(Lifts the revolver.)* If you do that, I'll use this. I want a new life, James. And for that I need resources. In exchange for the King's money, I shall give you this photograph. *(She now produces the photograph.)* So simple, really. A man and woman beside the sea. But from one image, a thousand complications are born.
LARRABEE. Give it to me and I'll get you the money.
IRENE ADLER. I heard Moriarty — the money is not yours to give.
LARRABEE. Irene, listen to me —
IRENE ADLER. *(Overlapping.)* How long will you let Moriarty

treat you like a child? Why not turn the tables on him?
LARRABEE. What are you saying?
IRENE ADLER. When Holmes arrives with the money, tell him you have the photograph. When he asks to see it — direct him to that closet, where I'll be waiting. And when Moriarty appears — *(Aiming the revolver toward the door.)* — I'll give him what he deserves.
LARRABEE. You wouldn't.
IRENE ADLER. I've shot tenors, James. After that, a woman can shoot anything. We shall divide the money equally. You'll be rid of Moriarty. I'll be free to start my new life. *(Holmes is heard, approaching —)*
HOLMES' VOICE. *(From off.)* Miss Adler?
IRENE ADLER. Well, James? *(Holmes is now knocking on the door.)*
HOLMES' VOICE. *(From off.)* Miss Adler — are you there?
IRENE ADLER. Do you want to be your own man or not?
LARRABEE. I do. *(Irene Adler vanishes into the closet, just as — Holmes pushes open the main door.)* Good evening, Mr. Holmes. You're right on time.
HOLMES. And you're not the person I've come for. I received a letter from Miss Adler regarding the photograph.
LARRABEE. The photograph is now in my possession.
HOLMES. She mentioned nothing of the sort.
LARRABEE. This is a recent development.
HOLMES. Like the twitch in your left eye.
LARRABEE. Pardon me?
HOLMES. It seems to wander in the direction of that closet.
LARRABEE. In fact, it does, and here is why: You will find the photograph waiting there.
HOLMES. And Miss Adler — what has become of her?
LARRABEE. I'm not at liberty to say. *(Holmes stares at him for a moment, then steps toward the closet —)* But, first, Mr. Holmes — I shall need to see the money. Have you brought the full amount?
HOLMES. It shall arrive any moment. My associate, Doctor Watson, is bringing it.
LARRABEE. But, you were told to come alone! *(Moriarty enters, followed by Sid Prince.)*
MORIARTY. Mr. Holmes — what a pleasure.
HOLMES. I find it a great disappointment. After a long ride in a shuttered cab — I thought you'd show me something new.
MORIARTY. You've been here before?

HOLMES. I nabbed one of Mr. Prince's cronies in this room — a safe-cracker, name of Colvin. He was hiding in that closet. We dragged him out by the heels.
SID PRINCE. Never heard o' 'im before.
HOLMES. Well, you certainly never heard of him after.
MORIARTY. Times have changed, Mr. Holmes.
HOLMES. Indeed they have. I see you're no longer using the room for counterfeiting. *(Holmes begins to inspect the room.)* All the cracks and crevices — they seem to have been sealed with caulk. How long did that take you, Mr. Prince?
SID PRINCE. I don't for a minute know wha' yer speakin' of.
HOLMES. Odd, then — that the same caulk is there, on your knees.
SID PRINCE. Wha's that you say?
HOLMES. With a woman, the sleeve of her blouse always implicates her. With a man: the knees of his trousers.
MORIARTY. *(With admiration.)* You are overmatched, Mr. Prince.
HOLMES. It's certain that the gas — once released — will never escape. Nor will the man tied to that chair with this rope. *(Holmes tosses the rope to Prince.)* Once our transaction is complete: You will take my money and leave me for dead.
MORIARTY. Once again, Mr. Holmes, your deduction is accurate —
HOLMES. Thank you so much.
MORIARTY. — However, there will be no transaction.
HOLMES. But Mr. Larrabee assured me if I stepped into that closet, I would find the missing photograph.
MORIARTY. Larrabee —
HOLMES. In fact, I think I shall do so now.
MORIARTY. — What is he talking about?!
LARRABEE. *(Desperate.)* Not until we see the money! *(Holmes turns toward the door —)*
HOLMES. As you wish — *(— And Watson peeks his head into the room.)*
WATSON. Holmes?
MORIARTY. Who's this?!
HOLMES. Watson — come in, come in. *(Watson steps into the room — closing the door fully behind him. He carries the valise.)*
WATSON. Good evening.
HOLMES. We were just discussing a neat little plan to asphyxiate me.
LARRABEE. *(Re: the valise.)* Is the money in there?
HOLMES. Of course it is. *(Holmes takes the valise from Watson and*

sets it on the table — still locked and unopened.) Here we are. And, while we're at it: Here's my revolver. *(He sets his revolver on the table. The others look on in amazement.)* I've no use for it. Shots could be heard in the alley — right, Professor? *(Holmes starts toward the closet —)* And now, if you'll excuse me, I shall retrieve the photograph.
WATSON. Holmes —
HOLMES. Don't worry, Watson. There's nothing to fear. *(— and he vanishes inside. Moriarty, Larrabee and Prince turn to each other quickly, as — Watson remains near the far wall.)*
MORIARTY. *(Whispered, to Larrabee.)* Larrabee — this was not the plan!
LARRABEE. I got his gun away from him, didn't I?!
SID PRINCE. But the closet is full of 'em!
LARRABEE. And there's your money — just like you asked. *(Moriarty goes to the valise, and — Sid Prince grabs Holmes' revolver, just as — A cry is heard from the closet —)*
HOLMES' VOICE. *(From off.)* NNNNNOOOOOOO!

SID PRINCE.	MORIARTY.
Wha's that?!	Get in there!

WATSON. *(Overlapping.)* Holmes! *(Holmes emerges from the closet. In his arms, he carries the limp and lifeless body of Irene Adler. Quietly:)* Oh, my God …
HOLMES. *(His heart breaking.)* Do you know something, Watson? … I've long imagined this moment. Since first I heard Miss Adler's Cleopatra — when, upon her death, she is carried onstage — and the tenor begins to sing a heartbreaking, unforgettable aria: *"Fino a domani"* … "Until tomorrow" … *(He gently lays the body of Irene Adler on the table, near the lamp.)* Since that moment I've imagined what it must feel like for a man to lose the woman of his dreams … *(During the following: Holmes removes his cloak and covers her body and face.)*
LARRABEE. What have you done to her?!
HOLMES. I should ask that of you, Mr. Larrabee. Was it not enough to deceive her and break her heart? Was it also necessary to suffocate her — to snuff out the life she placed so willingly in your hands?!
LARRABEE. That's a lie — I never touched her!
SID PRINCE. See there! I knew we couldn't trust 'im!
MORIARTY. Shut up — both of you!
HOLMES. *(To Larrabee.)* Your cries of innocence fail to account for this — *(Holmes produces the "J.L." handkerchief from his pocket.)*

I found it stuffed in her mouth. The monogram upon it, Mr. Larrabee, is yours.
LARRABEE. THAT'S IMPOSSIBLE.
MORIARTY. QUIET. *(Sid Prince lifts Holmes' revolver and aims it at Holmes —)*
SID PRINCE. NOW, CAN I PLUG 'IM ONE?
MORIARTY. NO GUNS.
HOLMES. It was my plan, Professor, to witness your crimes first-hand, to be the star witness at your trial ... but now I see there's no need. I don't plan to testify. In fact, I don't plan to leave this room, at all.

| WATSON. | SID PRINCE. |
| What? | Come again? |

HOLMES. What purpose could it serve to go out that door? *(Re: Watson.)* For gathered here, in one room, are my most trusted friend ... *(Re: Moriarty.)* My most formidable adversary ... *(Re: Irene Adler.)* And the first, and last, great love of my life ...
MORIARTY. *(Suspicious.)* What are you getting at, Holmes? *(Holmes holds a small key in the air. He does a series of gestures, which seem to relate to the matter he's discussing with the men ...)*
HOLMES. This is the key. It will open the valise. *(Illustrating.)* The key must be turned several times in a counter-clockwise manner — like so. (... *But these gestures are in fact meant for Watson, who stands behind the others, near the flywheel. In short: Holmes is signaling Watson to turn the flywheel and release the gas. Once Watson understands the plan — he nods — and, unknown to the others, silently turns the flywheel ... releasing the gas.)* Please make sure the King has sent the money in full. *(Moriarty nods to Prince — who takes the key and opens the valise. It is filled with bank notes.)*
MORIARTY. Well?
SID PRINCE. Looks to all be 'ere. *(A hissing sound begins to be heard.)*
HOLMES. Very good. That's done. *(Holmes now produces the photograph.)* Now the King may marry his princess with no fear of scandal. For this photograph — like everyone in this room and yours truly, as well — shall soon be nothing but ash. *(Holmes places the photograph atop Irene's body, as — the hissing sound grows louder.)*
LARRABEE. What's that sound? — That hissing?
MORIARTY. Prince — ?
SID PRINCE. *(Re: Watson.)* He's turned the gas on! I can smell it!
MORIARTY. TURN IT OFF! *(Larrabee races for the flywheel —*

it is, of course, locked open.)
LARRABEE. I can't budge it — it's LOCKED! *(Holmes begins loading his pipe.)*
MORIARTY. THE DOOR — GET IT OPEN!
HOLMES. Watson — do you have a light?
WATSON. Yes, sir. *(Holmes lifts the match — which freezes Moriarty and the others.)*
MORIARTY. Holmes — you wouldn't.
HOLMES. *(Re: his pipe.)* Yes — I know — it is a dangerous habit.
MORIARTY. *(Desperate.)* Listen to me —
HOLMES. But, as you know: *(Holmes prepares to light the match.)* Danger is part of my trade. *(Then, a series of things at once: Holmes lights the match, as — the men scream: "NO!" and — Irene Adler sits up and tosses the cloak over the electric lamp, which sends the room into complete darkness, as — various shouts and screams and gunshots are heard, as well as — bodies and footsteps scrambling about in the darkness — the table overturned — and then, just as suddenly: The electric lamp is uncovered. The room is lit once again, revealing: Moriarty, Larrabee and Sid Prince — all newly disheveled and bruised — lifting themselves from the ground. As for Holmes, Irene Adler and Watson — they are gone. The briefcase filled with money — gone. Holmes' revolver — gone. The door — open.)*
SID PRINCE. It din't blow! ... I smelled the gas — why on earth din't it blow?!
MORIARTY. Where's the money?
SID PRINCE. Gone. *(Larrabee is looking on the table for the photograph —)*
MORIARTY. And the photograph?
LARRABEE. Gone.
MORIARTY. *(To Sid Prince.)* Any sign of them out there?!
SID PRINCE. *(At the doorway.)* Gone.
LARRABEE. It can't be! *(Moriarty turns, viciously, to Larrabee —)*
MORIARTY. *(A threat.)* I told you, Larrabee: That woman will be the death of you. *(Watson, alone.)*
WATSON. *(Breathlessly.)* And off we raced! — Out the building and toward the street — whereupon we gathered in a nearby alley, awaiting a carriage. *(Under a street lamp. Holmes and Irene Adler enter.)*
HOLMES. Thrilling, wasn't it, Watson!
WATSON. Well — NO — you gave me quite a fright!
HOLMES. Miss Adler came up with much of the plan herself —
IRENE ADLER. Based on a scene from a Spanish opera —

HOLMES. And we improvised the rest, right there on the spot!
WATSON. But the gas? — How did you —
HOLMES. The chemical mixture on the rags — hidden in the valise — replicated the smell of gas perfectly.
WATSON. But the flywheel?! — the valve that released the gas?! — when you lit that match, we could have all been —
HOLMES. Before I answer, Watson, you must once again confess yourself utterly taken aback.
WATSON. I am! I confess it!
HOLMES. I ought to make you sign a paper to that effect.
WATSON. Why?
HOLMES. Because when I tell you the answer you will slap your hand to your forehead and announce that it is all so absurdly simple.
WATSON. I'll do nothing of the kind.
HOLMES. Very well, then. The gas line enters the building through a pipe in the alley. This afternoon I sent a man to cap the line — leaving nothing but air to flow through the pipes. *(Watson stares at Holmes, then claps his hand to his forehead —)*
WATSON. It's so ABSURDLY SIMPLE.
IRENE ADLER. *(With admiration.)* Indeed it is.
HOLMES. Now, Watson — we must hurry to the train station. Do you have the instructions I gave you?
WATSON. *(Producing the paper.)* Indeed, I do.
HOLMES. Ignore them. I have a new plan. One that will see us safely out of London — and on our way to Switzerland — where, on the eve of his wedding, we shall return the photograph, and complete our business with the King. You are to secure two seats on the first train to Paris — making certain to book them under an alias — as well as overland passage to the Swiss Alps. Is that clear?
WATSON. *(Starts off.)* Two seats to Paris. Right away.
IRENE ADLER. Three seats. *(Watson stops.)*
WATSON. Pardon me?
IRENE ADLER. Please book passage for three, Doctor Watson.
HOLMES. That's not necessary. *(To Watson.)* Two shall suffice.
IRENE ADLER. *(To Watson.)* But three are required.
HOLMES. *(More strongly.)* Listen to me, Watson: two seats —
IRENE ADLER. *(To Watson.)* Three —
HOLMES. But, Miss Adler —
IRENE ADLER. *(Overlapping.)* — And I won't hear another word about it. *(Standoff: Holmes and Irene staring at one another.)*

HOLMES. Watson, would you please inform Miss Adler that our journey is one of grave danger.

WATSON. Yes, of course —

IRENE ADLER. And would you please explain to Mr. Holmes that I, too, have unfinished business with the King — and no amount of danger shall dissuade me.

WATSON. Very well, but —

HOLMES. Miss Adler, you must understand: My work — and with it, perhaps, my life — is nearly done. And you needn't involve yourself in the final chapter. The scandal in Bohemia has been averted. The case is solved.

IRENE ADLER. And you must understand this: A woman may be courted and wed, captured and won ... but she can, Mr. Holmes, never be *solved*. *(Beat, turns to Watson.)* Three seats, Doctor Watson.

WATSON. *(A smile.)* Right away. *(A train whistle blows, and a light instantly isolates — Watson, alone. He holds a small valise.)* Within the hour I had secured our tickets. As for Holmes and Miss Adler — by taking a series of cabs and carriages through the city, they managed to avoid being followed by Moriarty's men. We boarded the train in the nick of time. *(Train whistle blows, again, as — lights expand to reveal a simple bench, which will serve as — the train compartment. Holmes and Irene Adler arrive.)*

HOLMES. We've cut it rather fine, haven't we? *(Calmly points out window.)* In fact, look there: the Professor himself.

WATSON. *(In terror.)* Moriarty!

HOLMES. *(With a laugh.)* Another minute and he'd have been on board with us! *(Holmes removes the silver cigarette case from his pocket.)* Cigarette, Watson?

WATSON. *(Still shaken.)* No, thank you. *(Holmes offers one to Irene — which she takes. They light up.)* Moriarty knows we're on this train?!

HOLMES. Remarkable, isn't he?

WATSON. But what will we do?!

IRENE ADLER. The question, I think, is what will *he* do? *(Holmes and Watson turn to her.)* Knowing this train will make one stop — at Canterbury — before arriving at Dover, Moriarty will no doubt engage a "special."

HOLMES. Precisely.

IRENE ADLER. An express train that will arrive in Dover —

HOLMES. And, hence, Paris —

IRENE ADLER. — Before we do.

WATSON. But then what will we do? *(Holmes turns to Irene, expectant.)*
IRENE ADLER. When our train stops in Canterbury — we will disembark —
HOLMES. — Make the cross-country journey to Folkstone —
IRENE ADLER. — And then cross the channel by boat to Dieppe.
HOLMES. Moriarty will continue onto Paris —
IRENE ADLER. And as he waits, in vain, for our arrival — we will make our way to Brussels —
HOLMES. — Down through Luxembourg —
IRENE ADLER. — And on to Switzerland. *(Irene and Holmes smoke, satisfied.)*
WATSON. But, why not just have the man arrested now?
HOLMES. The roundup of Moriarty's men begins tonight. We mustn't nab the Professor before that time, for fear of tipping off his cronies —
WATSON. But surely we could —
HOLMES. *(Overlapping.)* In this way, when he returns to London, his enterprise will be destroyed and the police will be waiting for him. *(To Irene.)* Now, we must consult the map. *(Holmes and Irene silently study a map, as — a final train whistle blows.)*
WATSON. *(To the audience.)* All went according to plan. As we got off the train in Canterbury, we could see the smoke from the express train approaching behind us. As it sped through the station — carrying Moriarty safely away into the distance — Holmes turned to me and said:
HOLMES. *(Importantly.)* There remains but one final question.
WATSON. And what is that?
HOLMES. Shall we have lunch here or wait for the buffet in Folkstone? *(Watson, alone.)*
WATSON. We made our way to Brussels that night — taking rooms in a secluded hotel at the end of a dark street. *(Holmes arrives, holding a telegram.)*
HOLMES. Watson: I've news from London — a telegram from Inspector Lestrade. He informs me that the police have secured the entire gang, with the exception of Larrabee and the Professor.
WATSON. And what of them?
HOLMES. Larrabee, for the most part, was found buried in a quarry.
WATSON. "For the most part"?
HOLMES. His head was bobbing in the river.

WATSON. Good heavens. And what of Moriarty?

HOLMES. Vanished. It's believed he's on the loose, somewhere on the Continent. And what's more: Our rooms on Baker Street were set afire.

WATSON. When?

HOLMES. Yesterday — only hours after we'd left.

WATSON. My God, Holmes! What will we do? *(A woman in mourning appears, carrying a large purse. Her face is covered by a black veil.)*

WOMAN IN MOURNING. *(To the men, as she weeps.)* Good sirs — there is no room! — no room for me at this hotel —

WATSON. *(Going to her immediately.)* Oh, I'm sorry to hear that.

WOMAN IN MOURNING. *(Overlapping.)* — My sister's funeral today — she's all I had left in the world! — and now nothing — and not a place to lay my head ...

HOLMES. *(To the woman.)* Take this money and see the concierge at the hotel on the city square. *(Holmes hands her the money. She opens her purse and begins to put the money inside, saying —)*

WOMAN IN MOURNING. Thank you, sir — you have a good heart ...

HOLMES. The concierge shall direct you across the street to the local jail — where you'll find a room awaiting you under the name — *(Holmes throws back her veil [or removes her hat completely], saying:)* — Madge Larrabee.

WATSON. What? *(The woman in mourning produces a revolver at the exact same moment that — a policeman apprehends her from behind, grabbing the gun away —)*

HOLMES. Thank you, Officer.

MADGE. CURSE YOU, SHERLOCK HOLMES.

HOLMES. I was sorry, Madge, to hear about the loss of both your brother and his head.

MADGE. I warned him about that songbird of his. Do you see where love can lead?!

HOLMES. A monstrous affliction. I quite agree. *(A police siren sounds, as — the policeman leads Madge away.)*

MADGE. Thanks to you, the Professor put a bounty on my head!

HOLMES. You needn't worry about him.

MADGE. *(Overlapping.)* He'll find you, Holmes! MARK MY WORDS: MORIARTY WILL FIND YOU! *(And she is gone. Holmes turns to Watson, who stands frozen in place.)*

HOLMES. I remind you, Watson, that I am a most dangerous

traveling companion. You must feel free, at any time, to return to London.

WATSON. Holmes —

HOLMES. *(From his heart.)* If any harm befell you, my friend ... I should never forgive myself. *(Watson turns to the audience.)*

WATSON. But I did not leave. In fact, at that moment I resolved to never leave Holmes' side till this danger had passed. *(Watson, alone. During the following: The stage, if possible, is gradually cleared of all but a tall, raised platform.)* For a charming week we wandered up the valley of the Rhone — our destination being the small village of Meiringen, nestled away in the Swiss Alps. *(Holmes appears, carrying his walking stick, as — the King of Bohemia, in his wedding vestments, appears opposite.)*

KING OF BOHEMIA. *(Buoyant.)* Sherlock Holmes — in the flesh! My wedding day is made!

HOLMES. I've brought the gift you desired.

KING OF BOHEMIA. Most excellent. *(Holmes produces the photograph, and hands it to the King —)* History shall thank you, Mr. Holmes, for your part in uniting the great houses of Europe ... *(— and, upon viewing it, the King's countenance changes ... tenderly, to the photo:)* Oh ... look at her ... how will ever I vanquish her from my heart...? *(Irene Adler has entered, opposite.)*

IRENE ADLER. *(Simply.)* Leave that to me.

KING OF BOHEMIA. *(Turning to see her.)* Irene...?

IRENE ADLER. I shall need your dagger. *(She approaches the King.)*

KING OF BOHEMIA. Pardon me?

IRENE ADLER. I have discovered, you see, that with the exception of Mr. Holmes, the heads of most men are mere appendages. *(She reaches into the King's leather belt — and removes a dagger.)* Therefore — *(She places her hands on the King's chest, near his heart —)*

KING OF BOHEMIA. No — please! *(— Then she takes the photograph from the King and places it upon his chest —)*

IRENE ADLER. — I shall give you what you so avidly seek: the absence of me. *(— And she lifts the dagger and cuts the photograph in half.)* There. *(She hands half of the photograph back to the King —)* Our business is completed. *(— And hands the other half to Holmes.)*

HOLMES. As is ours.

KING OF BOHEMIA. *(From his heart.)* I loved you, Irene.

IRENE ADLER. *(Simply.)* May you love your princess better. *(She leaves. Beat. The King turns to say something to Holmes, but before he can —)*

HOLMES. We require lodging, Your Highness. Something splendid and picturesque.
KING OF BOHEMIA. There is an inn at the village gate. And from there, you may follow the footpath to the falls.
WATSON. What falls are you speaking of?
HOLMES. Reichenbach Falls.
KING OF BOHEMIA. No trip here is complete without them. The crashing water. The tremendous abyss. *(Clutching his hand to his heart.)* An abyss deep and dark as a man's broken heart —
HOLMES. *(Impatient.)* Yes, yes, you've made your point —
WATSON. And may we then continue past the falls, and travel on to the next village?
KING OF BOHEMIA. No. The path is cut halfway around the falls — but does not continue across to the far side.
HOLMES. So a traveler must —
KING OF BOHEMIA. A traveler must always *return the same way that he came. (Watson, alone.)*
WATSON. The King arranged rooms for us at the inn. And Holmes insisted we visit the falls, at once. However, when I went to his room, he was nowhere to be found. From the corridor, I heard voices — they seemed to be coming from Miss Adler's room … *(In the brilliant light of a picture window. Holmes and Adler in the midst of a heated, passionate discussion.)*
IRENE ADLER. *(Sharp.)* No — the point is that for one full week we have traveled together — and each day you come to my door and stand in my room — and for what reason?! So you can tell me about your PIPES?
HOLMES. Miss Adler, please —
IRENE ADLER. Your brier and your amber stem and your before breakfast pipe?! — How you prefer your clay pipe when you're thinking and your cherry pipe when you're arguing —
HOLMES. Listen, now —
IRENE ADLER. Well, I should load that cherry pipe, Mr. Holmes, because the argument has just begun!
HOLMES. MIGHT I SPEAK?
IRENE ADLER. FOR WHAT REASON? To tell me once again about your article on "The Distinction Between the Ashes of Various Tobaccos"? —
HOLMES. First of all: It was not an "article" — it was a MONOGRAPH —
IRENE ADLER. Oh, I see.

HOLMES. — And furthermore it featured illustrations, in color, of over —
IRENE ADLER. — "Over one hundred types of tobacco" —
HOLMES. One hundred and FIFTY-THREE.
IRENE ADLER. I DON'T CARE, MR. HOLMES. Do you understand? Day after day I open my door to you, hoping to see some evidence of your heart ... some awareness of that which stands before you ... but in every case —
HOLMES. But, just yesterday I stood before you and spoke from my heart —
IRENE ADLER. — About medieval pottery, Stradivarius violins, and the Buddhism of Ceylon!
HOLMES. THEN WHAT IS A MAN TO SAY? Shall I ask Mr. Larrabee or the King? I suppose those paragons of heartbreak and deceit knew all the proper words to say to a woman?!
IRENE ADLER. *(Forcefully.)* In matters of love, at least: They were men of courage.
HOLMES. And I am NOT? *(Her stare gives him his answer. Silence.)* You have made your point. I shall come to your room no more. But, I should like — before I go — to show you something I've carried with me since the day we met. *(He produces a small book from an inside pocket.)*
IRENE ADLER. *(Seeing the title.)* Limestone: A Brief History ...?!
HOLMES. Filled with dazzling insights —
IRENE ADLER. You can't be serious!
HOLMES. — And also home to this. *(From the small book, he removes: a pressed flower — the white rose.)* This rose — you gave it to me on your wedding day.
IRENE ADLER. And you gave me its derivation.
HOLMES. I pressed it in this book, hoping one day I might return it to you.
IRENE ADLER. That's not necessary, Mr. Holmes —
HOLMES. And that is my point! We inherit many things on this earth — food and shelter, sunlight and rain — and all these things are necessary for our existence. But, a rose is not; a rose is *extra*. Like all human kindness — like love itself — a rose is not a condition of life ... but an embellishment of it.
IRENE ADLER. *(Testing him.)* Still, a man may live without it.
HOLMES. Or, he may begin to live for it. *(Pause. He is very close to her now.)*
IRENE ADLER. *(Not giving in.)* I'm afraid, Mr. Holmes, that in

your case I find that impossible.
HOLMES. And I'm afraid, Miss Adler ... *(Pause, finding the words.)* ... that when one has excluded the impossible ... whatever remains ... however improbable ... must be the truth. *(And they begin to kiss, as lights shift to — Watson, alone.)*
WATSON. Needless to say: I did not enter the room. Later that day, Holmes and I set out on foot — and within one hour we had reached Reichenbach Falls. *(Lights expand to reveal the tall platform, which will suggest the falls. Holmes, walking stick in hand, is climbing the steps which lead to the top of the platform, as — the sound of crashing water begins, growing louder throughout.)*
HOLMES. *(Awed by the sight.)* Remarkable, isn't it? A torrent of green water roaring foreverdown, into an immense chasm of coal-black rock — a roiling, clamoring pit of extraordinary depth. *(Beat.)* Come, Watson — we must walk the path to its end! *(Watson [who has not climbed the platform] takes a long look at Holmes — who continues to gaze, mesmerized, at the falls.)*
WATSON. *(To audience.)* And it was at that moment that a young Swiss man arrived.
YOUNG SWISS MAN. Are you Doctor Watson?
WATSON. Yes. *(Watson is handed a letter. The young Swiss man leaves.)*
HOLMES. What is it, Watson?
WATSON. The envelope bears the hotel insignia — *(Opening and reading it.)* It is from the innkeeper.
HOLMES. Yes, and?
WATSON. Miss Adler. She has fallen ill. The innkeeper fears she may have been poisoned.
HOLMES. Then there isn't much time —
WATSON. The local doctor is away — they've tried in vain to contact him, but —
HOLMES. You must go, Watson. I shall follow behind.
WATSON. But, Holmes —
HOLMES. You are a doctor — this is your greatest duty. You must go immediately to the aid of Miss Adler!
WATSON. *I won't leave you alone,* Holmes —
HOLMES. *(With force.)* And *why?* Because you fear my death? *(Before Watson can answer.)* Know this, Watson: If my book were closed tonight, I should not have lived in vain. *(Beat.)* Go now, my good doctor — go, and do not delay. *(Watson, alone.)*
WATSON. As I turned to leave, I observed him: standing alone,

gazing at those brutal waters. *(Beat.)* It was the last that I would ever see of him in this world. *(Irene Adler enters, opposite, holding a book — happy and content. Watson stops cold, confused, when he sees her —)* Miss Adler — what are you doing?
IRENE ADLER. *(Lightly.)* Attempting to read a book given to me by Mr. Holmes — however, I fear my interest in *Ancient Inuit Phrenology* is not what it should be.
WATSON. But — I don't understand — you're feeling well enough to sit outside?
IRENE ADLER. I've never felt better. *(Off Watson's look.)* What is it, Doctor?
WATSON. You were not taken ill?
IRENE ADLER. When? *(Watson holds out the letter.)*
WATSON. I was at the falls with Mr. Holmes — and an urgent letter arrived — saying you'd been poisoned — that you needed a doctor at once — it was a matter of great ... *(He stops. Watson's face goes blank. The reality of the situation hits both of them at once.)*
IRENE ADLER. *(Quietly.)* We've been deceived.
WATSON. Yes. *(Beat, then to the audience, urgently.)* We raced down the village street — Miss Adler at my side — and we made for the path which I had just traversed. One hour later, we found ourselves at Reichenbach Falls. *(Sound of rushing water, as before.)* There was no sign of Holmes. Only his walking stick.
IRENE ADLER. *(To Watson.)* Look there —
WATSON. And there, in the soft mud on the path, one could clearly see —
IRENE ADLER. — Not one set of footprints ... but two.
WATSON. Indeed, they were the steps of two men ... leading away, toward the very end of the path. *(Beat.)* There were no footprints returning.
IRENE ADLER. *(Calls out, terrified.)* HOLMES!
WATSON. *(Calls out, desperate.)* HOLMES!

IRENE ADLER.	WATSON.
ARE YOU THERE?!	HOLMES!

(Watson and Irene's voices are drowned out by the sound of the crashing water.)
WATSON. But there was no answer ... only our own voices ... echoing from the cliffs around us. When we returned to where Holmes had left his walking stick, I saw something gleaming amid the rocks. It was a silver cigarette case. *(Watson produces the cigarette case. He hands it to Irene, as — lights rise on: Holmes, atop the plat-*

form. Moriarty [perhaps] stands nearby — his back to the audience, his face as yet unseen.) Underneath the case was a piece of paper, torn from Holmes' notebook — and addressed to me:

HOLMES. My dear Watson, I write these lines through the courtesy of Professor Moriarty who patiently awaits the final discussion between us. As for the letter from the innkeeper, I was certain that it was a hoax — a fact the Professor has now confirmed — but, wanting only for your safety, I encouraged you to depart. I am sorry, Watson, that to vanquish my great enemy I must bring sorrow to you, my dearest friend. Please forgive me. And know that all is now in order. *(A look at Irene.)* I should like Miss Adler to keep my cigarette case. All I wish to say to her is written within. *(To Watson.)* Do give my greetings to your dear wife, and know me to forever be, very sincerely yours …

MORIARTY. *(Appearing/turning.)* Sherlock Holmes: Your path seems to have reached its end.

HOLMES. And yours as well. *(Holmes and Moriarty slowly step toward one another —)*

MORIARTY. I should be careful that you don't kill us both.

HOLMES. It is both, or none. *(— And at the very moment they begin to reach for each other: There is a final, tremendous rush of water, as — the light on Holmes and Moriarty snaps to black. Irene slowly opens the cigarette case.)*

WATSON. When Miss Adler opened the case, she found nothing but a small photograph — one edge still bearing the marks of a knife. On the back, in Holmes' own hand, were written these words …

IRENE ADLER. *(Reading, quietly.)* "Fino a domani."

WATSON. … And nothing more.

IRENE ADLER. "Until tomorrow." *(Watson, alone.)*

WATSON. Little now remains for me to tell. An examination by experts left no doubt that the fight between the two men ended in a reeling fall over the edge, locked in each other's arms; a final death grip which carried them down into the pounding waters … where they remain to this day: A generation's greatest criminal, and its foremost champion of law — together forever in the depths of that tremendous cauldron. That dreadful, watery abyss. *(Lights now reveal — a London street. Before dawn — identical to the beginning. The man with paper is revealed once again, standing under the glow of the lamppost, his face still fully concealed.)* It was obvious, of course, that a fall of that kind could not be survived; and that any

attempt to recover the bodies was hopeless. *(Beat.)* To which I can only imagine Holmes' reply—
MAN WITH PAPER. There is nothing, Watson, more deceptive than an obvious fact. *(Startled, Watson turns to see the man — who has not lowered the newspaper.)*
WATSON. *Holmes?! (Lights rush to black.)*

End of Play

PROPERTY LIST

Newspaper
Letters
Phonograph with cylinder
Garden trowel
Silver cigarette case
Red case of Moroccan leather with drug paraphernalia
Red rose
Gardening scissors
Notes
Bullets, revolver
Fireplace poker
Index cards
Bouquet of white flowers
Bible
Handkerchiefs
Luggage
Smoke rocket
Whistle
Walking stick
Leather bag with tools, stethoscope
Pistols
Notebook
Pipe, tobacco
Knife
Photograph
Breakfast remains
Pen and paper
Leather valise with money
Chemical supplies, beakers
Cigarettes
Rope
Matches
Telegram
Purse
Dagger
Book with pressed flower

SOUND EFFECTS

Soprano aria
Siren
Crash, loud sounds
Cheers
Fire bell
Police whistle
Hissing
Gunshots, screams, loud sounds
Train whistle
Waterfall

NEW PLAYS

★ **RABBIT HOLE by David Lindsay-Abaire.** Winner of the 2007 Pulitzer Prize. Becca and Howie Corbett have everything a couple could want until a life-shattering accident turns their world upside down. "An intensely emotional examination of grief, laced with wit." –*Variety.* "A transcendent and deeply affecting new play." –*Entertainment Weekly.* "Painstakingly beautiful." –*BackStage.* [2M, 3W] ISBN: 978-0-8222-2154-8

★ **DOUBT, A Parable by John Patrick Shanley.** Winner of the 2005 Pulitzer Prize and Tony Award. Sister Aloysius, a Bronx school principal, takes matters into her own hands when she suspects the young Father Flynn of improper relations with one of the male students. "All the elements come invigoratingly together like clockwork." –*Variety.* "Passionate, exquisite, important, engrossing." –*NY Newsday.* [1M, 3W] ISBN: 978-0-8222-2219-4

★ **THE PILLOWMAN by Martin McDonagh.** In an unnamed totalitarian state, an author of horrific children's stories discovers that someone has been making his stories come true. "A blindingly bright black comedy." –*NY Times.* "McDonagh's least forgiving, bravest play." –*Variety.* "Thoroughly startling and genuinely intimidating." –*Chicago Tribune.* [4M, 5 bit parts (2M, 1W, 1 boy, 1 girl)] ISBN: 978-0-8222-2100-5

★ **GREY GARDENS book by Doug Wright, music by Scott Frankel, lyrics by Michael Korie.** The hilarious and heartbreaking story of Big Edie and Little Edie Bouvier Beale, the eccentric aunt and cousin of Jacqueline Kennedy Onassis, once bright names on the social register who became East Hampton's most notorious recluses. "An experience no passionate theatergoer should miss." –*NY Times.* "A unique and unmissable musical." –*Rolling Stone.* [4M, 3W, 2 girls] ISBN: 978-0-8222-2181-4

★ **THE LITTLE DOG LAUGHED by Douglas Carter Beane.** Mitchell Green could make it big as the hot new leading man in Hollywood if Diane, his agent, could just keep him in the closet. "Devastatingly funny." –*NY Times.* "An out-and-out delight." –*NY Daily News.* "Full of wit and wisdom." –*NY Post.* [2M, 2W] ISBN: 978-0-8222-2226-2

★ **SHINING CITY by Conor McPherson.** A guilt-ridden man reaches out to a therapist after seeing the ghost of his recently deceased wife. "Haunting, inspired and glorious." –*NY Times.* "Simply breathtaking and astonishing." –*Time Out.* "A thoughtful, artful, absorbing new drama." –*Star-Ledger.* [3M, 1W] ISBN: 978-0-8222-2187-6

DRAMATISTS PLAY SERVICE, INC.
440 Park Avenue South, New York, NY 10016 212-683-8960 Fax 212-213-1539
postmaster@dramatists.com www.dramatists.com